Table of Contents

Overview

A UK resident has completed a book which explores and recommends answers to some of the psychological and other emotional problems experienced by women and girls.

Paul Tempest, 62, a former computer engineer has published "Anorexia in Girls - the Main Causes and the Best Cures".

This book details the fundamental cause of anorexia our most deadly of the mental illnesses which perhaps accounts for a half a million fatalities every year. For those with persistent anorexia about 20 percent die within 20 years and 10 percent die within 10 years, little is understood about anorexia beyond this book and the sufferers are simply classed as mentally ill.

However, this book explains the biology and fundamental causes of anorexia and the best ways to manage the condition and also the best cures. Anxiety and depression have not been overlooked and he has analysed the fundamental cause of each and the best solutions too.

Among the issues this book handles is the impact the digital revolution has had on young women, who end up damaged by conducting intense relationships online instead of in person.

Mr Tempest says this damage, known as Digital Indoctrination Fallout, manifests itself in conditions that cause self-harming, as well as suicidal thoughts.

He has explored mental illnesses for several years and had relationships with women who suffer from not only these conditions but conditions that include depression, bipolar, anorexia and anxiety. This book, unlike others, does not have to rely on case studies as such as all of the examples provided are from actual relationships he has engaged in himself.

These relationships now help to make a substantial insight into the mental illnesses women have to cope with and the analysis that has been brought to bear is astounding in his clinical assessment of both the conditions that drive the mental illnesses and the cause of the illnesses and the potential routes to correct them.

These relationships were conducted online and were very rewarding and enjoyable with women that often have to struggle to cope with daily life, it gave him a huge reward just by being able to work with them and help them find better solutions to their daily trauma.

The book itself has taken over a year to write and was never actually an intention from the outset, he was convinced by medical staff that his knowledge was crucial in the fight against mental illness for women and a book needed to be written to share his experiences and conclusions.

These conclusions are drawn from a detailed analysis of his relationships and experiences with many women that suffer from the mental illnesses with only a small number of examples actually being recorded in the book that demonstrate particular aspects of the conditions.

This is the first book to identify Digital Indoctrination and subsequent fallout (especially by pop stars and gaming) as the principle cause of suicidal thoughts in girls. This condition is generated by causing an emotionally high state that is artificial in nature and not like that of a genuine relationship which is expected by Mother Nature. These relationships can then be easily broken and concluded unexpectedly and leave the participant with withdrawal symptoms and emotional trauma.

Digital relationships of this nature can easily be created by pop stars who use multimedia techniques to drive an emotional connection with their fans. Gone are the days of the odd magazine article and posters, now they talk directly to their supports and generate a huge emotional commitment from their followers, often in their millions. These emotional highs and the unrealistic expectations in life that go with them are a dangerous cocktail to leave substantial emotional trauma.

Gaming is another multimedia source that can drive obsessional behaviour with huge emotional drives and too can generate substantial emotional highs that are not born out of a real relationship as expected by Mother Nature. Again, a sudden break in this behaviour can cause self-harming and suicidal thoughts to materialise as withdrawal symptoms born out of a huge frustration and emotional trauma are generated when this is suddenly removed.

Girls are just not mentally prepared for this type of emotional commitment and then an unexpected termination of that emotional commitment, severe trauma can follow and that drives the self-harming and suicidal thoughts and in some cases attempted suicides and actual suicides. This can happen to young women and girls who never knew what was going to happen to them and the potential mental injury that could occur.

This is now a huge problem in society and he has estimated that as many as half a million girls a month may now be impacted by Digital Indoctrination Fallout globally, which equates to well over 25,000 girls becoming new victims in the US every month and well over 7,000 every month in the UK.

Furthermore there are substantial rises in the numbers of girls that are reporting self-harming which has reached nearly 20% of girls in the 16-24 age group and these figures are still rising every year with no peak in sight. It is no coincidence that this sharp escalation has happened in step with the rise in digital technology and Mr Tempest has been able to put his 30 years' experience in IT to good use here.

If we do not take action to manage our emotion commitments and reduce online relationships these figures could easily reach 30% of our young women. There is no medication available for this condition and emotional management techniques are required to handle this type of emotional trauma. Because these conditions are relationship driven many of the techniques explored are also sexual in nature.

The book has also analysed two fundamental bonding systems that are used by females to drive their emotional connections with their relationships and how in one of these bonding systems a failure can cause self-harming and suicidal thoughts. A failure in the other bonding system is the cause of mental health illnesses such as anorexia, depression, anxiety and bipolar.

This book is not only the first book to identify Digital Indoctrination Fallout it goes much further and it is also being the first book to identify that the sustained digital emotional heightening that causes obsessions can cause other mental illnesses too.

Here he has identified that sustained digital emotional heightening can be the direct cause of other illnesses like anorexia and the bipolar disorder too and maybe the reason that a recent survey in the UK showed that nearly 25% of 14 year old girls had suffered emotional trauma and had incurred depression.

For those with persistent anorexia about 20 percent die within 20 years and 10 percent die within 10 years and little is understood about anorexia beyond this book. However, this book explains the fundamental causes of anorexia and the best ways to manage the condition and also the best cures. Due to the vast experience of Mr Tempest he is also able to detail the fundamental biology and the best solutions to overcome some of our other mental illnesses too.

Currently women and girls with conditions like anorexia have to endure the stigma of mental health issues and they are not sufficiently supported by society and yet this is a simple emotional problem that is often caused by others now in the digital world through excessive emotional heightening.

Not only is anorexia on the rise but there are worrying signs that young teenage girls are being exposed to bipolar conditions very early in their life and this is also being caused by others now in the digital world through excessive emotional heightening.

He has analysed the fundamental cause for depression and anxiety and these too have a full explanation and the best solutions, with information for rape victims too. This book goes still further and he has also detailed the fundamental cause of bulimia and OCD and the relationship between these illnesses and the best cures for these as well.

These mental illnesses are then compared with other known conditions like drug abuse, alcoholism and gambling addictions and their similarities lead to surprising conclusions and also includes a full description of narcissism, it's importance and how it impacts our bonding and our lives and it's relationship with PTSD victims who suffer from these bonding failures.

This book has revolutionised the emotional connections with mental health issues and old ideas will have to change. This book is a true leader in the fight against mental health issues and emotional care.

Introduction

The following is a result of five years' research and has taken over a year to write, working with women who have suffered medical trauma because of events that are often beyond their control. Depression, Bipolar, Anorexia, Anxiety, Frustration, Self-Harming and Suicidal Thoughts were amongst the serious medical conditions that I would not like to try and cope with in life myself, but they had to. The conditions I encountered are often referred to as a group known as BPD or Borderline Personality Disorder.

I will start by introducing you to how our worship bonding systems work and then progress though the equilibrium bonding process and show how these work including the issues we get when these fail to work normally and the emotional impact this has on us and also include the potential solutions to return us to a happy state. This analysis will include a lot of raw biology and you should be prepared to accept it for what it is and then you can fully understand what your options are. So there is a warning here, this book contains human biology, the female breeding cycle and emotional management techniques and you should not read this book if you will be offended by those.

In the US anorexia has the highest fatality rate of any mental illness and eating disorders are a daily struggle for 10 million females (1 million men) with the figures predicting 1.5 million women suffering from anorexia and around 2.5 million women suffering from bulimia with the binge eating disorders accounting for the rest, around 6 million women.

Anorexia is a terrible illness to live with as it restricts the victims eating capability causing them to vomit after meals, sometimes hours after they have eaten. These sufferers often find themselves eating very light meals during a prolonged anorexic spell in order to get some nourishment. Commonly they will eat things like fish and sugary items in order to generate some energy, ice cream is also a favourite. This book will demonstrate that anorexia is a part of our bonding systems and also discuss the best cures for anorexia too.

I have had several relationships with women that have suffered those conditions and there was a common theme amongst their problems, they clearly had bonding issues and their emotions were often in turmoil. I investigated further and what I found was surprising. The conditions I encountered are often referred to as a group known as BPD or Borderline Personality Disorder and this book will look at the anorexia condition in detail.

Back in our history we used our worship bonding to join together and manage our lives as a group; we were tribal and looked to the tribal leader to provide security and food. They would organise our day to day lives and oversee our breeding commitments. As we are monkeys there was a natural way to organise this, we could work together using our worship bonding processes which enable us to group together and respond to the needs of the group.

The tribal leaders would organise all sorts of worship rituals to make us worship him and through him the group joined together. We would sing and perform acts of worship like slaughtering and offer this to the gods as a sacrifice. This savagery activated our bonding by bringing us together in a shared moment to worship and this worship was maintained throughout our lives.

As the worship bonding was maintained throughout our lives it helped create the very cause for our existence and once that cause was established we needed that cause to exist. If we separated from the tribal group, we could not mentally manage on our own as our bonding had been set to a tribal group and we needed that bonding to continue to function normally. We could join another tribe of course and worship with them, but worship had become a fundamental part of our lives and it needed to be maintained or we would not function properly and start to become unstable. We would be emotionally unbalanced due to the lack of security, the issues around finding and providing food and the unstable breeding conditions.

Today worship is not as dramatic and does not evoke the same strong feelings as our tribal leaders could evoke in us, who bound us together in an unbreakable bond. Then we could fight and feed the tribe at his command, live where he wanted us to live and run our lives by his council. We lived and died through his leadership and that leadership was absolute.

We still know how to worship of course but it is a meagre shadow of how we used to live and it no longer triggers the same narcissistic bonding that totally governed our lives, which our ancestors were able to utilise. These days we tend to think of that as indoctrination and it is most notably used to create suicide bombers of course. It is used to fuse our brains to a cult or doctrine and sets our worship bonding processes and once that is complete it must be maintained, just as in our ancestors, or if it is withdrawn we become mentally and emotionally unstable.

As you can see it is relatively straight forward to create a suicide bomber, once the worship bonding has been accomplished all you need to do is withdraw or forbid the worship and let the mental instability set in. This will cause a huge frustration in the nervous system which is difficult to deal with and can cause self-harming, as this condition grows a feeling of worthlessness persists and we eventually become suicidal. Then they can offer a reward that will gratify the worship and this act will restore all of their beliefs in life and the very purpose for their life will be justified. Of course, it is important never to place your life in the hands of those that would harm you and perpetrate such a despicable act.

This indoctrination process has been used in some of our societies of course, and Pol Pot was a most notable tyrant that was able to generate genocide in Cambodia. Other cults also rely on being able to set our worship bonding process to enable them to dominate and control our lives.

In our current societies we often see worship bonding being set in our soldiers. Often young males will obsess about becoming a soldier from an early age and this obsession has already done the work of the indoctrination process. Soldiers will enter the combat arena with their worship bonding set and this will enable them to commit huge acts of bravery as their worship dominates their mental state. Worship enables that to happen, it creates a mental state that is totally dominated by the worship values and joins the soldiers together with their worship bonding so they can act as a combined group.

The problem for soldiers of course is when they stop being soldiers and they hang up their weapons. As their worship bonding was set it needs to be maintained, just as in our ancestors and this can only be done via obsession or indoctrination again to give them a new worship value just as it did in our ancestors.

Soldiers do not find this an easy thing to do; the cause for their life has vanished abruptly without a cause to justify keeping their life going. Such a worship bonding failure is severe and it generates pressure on the nervous system which Mother Nature provides to ensure we maintain our worship at all costs to keep our purpose in life. Veteran soldiers often find a new cause for their life impossible to find and fight the condition, sometimes for years, before it overwhelms them and they commit suicide. In the US it has been stated that the veteran suicide rate is 20 people every single day in a recent presidential speech. The annual global suicide rate has been estimated at around 800,000, so nearly 20 times that of the annual US suicide rate, so perhaps as many as 400 veterans commit suicide every single day.

Of course it is not only soldiers that suffer in our society, these days we have a totally new phenomenon called digital technology. Such is the power of this technology it can easily generate an obsession or indoctrination just like our ancestor's tribal leader. It can bring incredibly powerful thought processes and place them directly in our brains and set our worship bonding.

If you are suffering from suicidal thoughts it is best to look at what has caused an obsession in your life or perhaps something has generated an indoctrination process. Once this is withdrawn you will get a worship bonding failure and you must look to repair your worship bonding to become mentally stable again, failure to find a solution will lead to the same fate as the veteran soldiers here.

I will now fully analyse a woman's bonding and demonstrate what the solutions can be.

Our Life with Emotions

Life is an amazing thing; we exist through a series of bodily functions which have been given to us by Mother Nature. Some are mandatory like our heart beat, brain activity and breathing, but after that our life is then driven by our emotions. Some of these are fundamental to our existence and when they are activated they become necessary for our life and they facilitate our security, eating and breeding.

The other emotions are ours to help us govern our life. Yes, we love our pleasures in life, driven by our senses like sight, taste, hearing, touch and smell. We respond to these to generate our emotions of excitement or sadness, comfort or fear and we can experience dozens of others too.

Our emotions are our life force and the fundamental ones Mother Nature has given us are worship to drive our security, to create our ability to act with others and hunt or defend ourselves. We like to acclaim our purpose in life and our ancestors used worship with sacrifices to signify our right to exist above that of other species.

We need to eat and hunger is essential to ensure that we feed ourselves at regular intervals and to create a family unit bonding is also essential to ensure we breed. After that we live to please ourselves and each other but we cannot govern the emotions that Mother Nature has given us to ensure the survival of the human race. When they become active they stay with for the rest of our lives.

Our emotions work in perfect balance, a bit like our bodies they are an incredible feet of engineering. For every emotion we have, there is an opposite emotion that enables us to always generate an emotional balance and if that balancing process fails and we go out of balance, then we suffer from emotional trauma. But there are some exceptions though, when we activate Mother Nature's special emotions, things work slightly differently.

Feeling hungry and feeling full up are opposites and balance each other out eventually but the hunger is quelled immediately we start eating and feeling full is to stop us eating any more. They are more task and completion emotions.

That is how it is with the with Mother Nature's life force emotions, she wants us to complete our missions and then accept we have achieved the desired results. It is the same with a manic episode when we get extra sexual thoughts, the breeding side of ourselves is not completing its mission and we need orgasms to exhaust the manic emotions. When our emotions swing with a bipolar condition there is a hypomanic and manic (high) side and depression which is the low side.

Such is the power of a strong orgasm it will reset and rebalance all of our emotions. Weak orgasms do not always achieve this and that is normally due to poor partnership bonding and poor foreplay techniques that cause a lack of emotional rebalancing which is needed for our emotional health.

Worship is also a task and completion emotion but it cannot be balanced or exhausted, it needs to be maintained. When we use worship and indoctrination it sets an unending task which we have to resolve every day, and that remains until we replace that worship with another form of worship. Our beliefs in life are very much a part of us.

Failure to complete our life force tasks and emotions leads to severe consequences that are dealt out as punishments by Mother Nature. Worship as our most powerful emotion can also be used in conjunction with other emotions to intensify them and then manipulate the way those emotions are balanced, like bravery might be intensified when human sacrifice might be needed when we go to war. But once activated failure to maintain our worship leads to us becoming emotionally unstable, our worship cannot be allowed to fail as it is a life force emotion which will cause severe emotional trauma and a catastrophic emotional breakdown. This can often become a suicidal condition for those that are exposed to such an event.

For our breeding a key emotion is embarrassment, when we blush because of self-humiliation in front of others. But that humiliation changes totally in front of our partners. It makes us feel sexy; we nibble ears and squeeze ass cheeks as we melt into our partner's arms. As the bodily play and accepted embarrassment and humiliation increases our desire for sex which becomes ever more intense as the foreplay continues towards the main event. Intercourse can be a passionate affair that partners revel in as they enjoy each other's company.

But that desire is restricted, normally to a woman's bonded partner, and the bonding process is essential for her breeding success. Bonding is an essential part of Mother Nature's breeding programme and ensures that the breeding cycle can be maintained down the generations. Worship, our most powerful emotion is used to start the bonding process with a girl's crush and a bonding obsession also has the ability to force a bonding process whenever it is used as it can manipulate and intensify other emotions.

Worship and indoctrination are incredibly powerful forces that manipulate our minds and if worship is engaged and then withdrawn again we can become severely emotionally unbalanced, even to the point of suicide. Mother Nature has organised our feelings and our emotions to ensure we complete our survival obligations, and she has forced that upon us.

You will see that worship has not been designed to be a solitary activity and it is connected to our bonding, it will set our belief system, reduce our current bonding and add in a new high priority bonding. This enables our soldiers to go off and fight and forfeit their lives for example. However, when we obsess over something and invoke worship there is not always an associated valid bonding to substitute and this has the unusual effect of depleting our bonding but without the substitute bonding and leaving someone effectively unbonded, or forcing selfish and aloof people to bond with themselves.

When a woman becomes unbonded she is then exposed to a Bipolar condition as her emotions swing. Bonding is needed because it helps maintain and stabilise our emotions, gives us security and it is also a fundamental part of Mother Nature's breeding cycle.

People who worship and then bond with themselves are single minded, self-centred and aloof are seen as brats. Because a brat has set their bonding by worship they will always need to maintain that worship or modify and replace that bonding by worship when they get a new partner. Failure to modify their bonding by using worship correctly can lead to a worship bonding failure as their belief system will be compromised in a new partnership if they do fail to maintain their worship correctly. If a new partner cannot accept female worship to allow her to complete her bonding the failure is pre-destined.

That's how we work, and the following will demonstrate how Mother Nature can and does force us to do her work.

In order to learn emotional management techniques I needed to learn BDSM as that was the human experience of manipulating our breeding emotions and orgasms and that would hold the answers to exploring the impact of emotional trauma. I joined a few BDSM sites and started to learn about the Dominant male and the Master, and how women used their emotional submission to generate their orgasms.

I was chatting to dozens of women now, all about their feelings and how it impacted their orgasms, and exactly what their bonding was giving them. It was not long before the pieces started to come together, how humiliation (private sexual play) triggered their bonding to the male and then their submission triggered their orgasm. How more extreme humiliation play could increase their enjoyment and negative emotions made things even hotter, like being forced to mimic an animal or being punished. The more they could submit to the male the bigger their orgasm.

This was all a part of Mother Nature's breeding cycle and her bonding process to establish a mate and breed successfully.

Now the pieces were in place I could start to explore and prove some theories.

A Woman's Bonding

So my journey was under way, I needed to find out why some women seemed to bond and anchor their bonding equilibrium centre point to their partner and enjoy a good sex life and good orgasms with their partner and why others did not bond, did not anchor their equilibrium point and had emotional difficulties in life. I had relationships with quite a few submissive females online and carefully started to work things out.

A submissive is someone who submits to emotional stimulation and manipulation by a dominant or Master and this will often include sexual emotional management which generates our most intense emotions. Reaching a climax allows us to exhaust our pent up emotions and regain our emotional balance when Mother Nature uses emotional calming to conclude these activities.

These women included a couple of women that had previously attempted suicide, alpha females, sluts, women with depression, hypomanic and manic episodes, anxiety and anorexia and two that had been raped. What I discovered was quite remarkable.

What became clear is that our emotional state is heavily linked to our bonding and breeding systems and there is clear governance of our emotions and emotional state from our bonding and breeding systems which is a principle actor for our emotional state.

Women have a bonding equilibrium pendulum which hangs close to the centre for most females. When they meet their male partner their equilibrium point anchors to their partner and they accept his sexual arousal and then orgasm for him. It is the part of the bonding process and it is driven by our emotions and also our belief system, which is set by experience. When our belief system is set and our bonding equilibrium set these two halves come together in the bonding process that we call love.

Our equilibrium strengthens as our bonding develops and our belief systems strengthen and joins us to our partner because of our bonding fulfilment. When our partner matches our sexual tastes, our arousal is just right and our euphoria and orgasms are perfect for breeding. If you enjoy being taken or rough sex and you need higher levels of euphoria and a lot of sexual stimulation this will depend on your emotional boundaries which are separate from your bonding equilibrium.

But things these days don't always work like that. Girls don't start to breed as soon as Mother Nature intended, and masturbation and sexual play has become popular as it's a good emotional release. In this instance your bonding equilibrium is not secure because it cannot strengthen if there is no bonding fulfilment and your belief system is not supporting your breeding.

What we see below is how our emotional state is regulated by our bonding systems as they are our principle system for emotional management and the bonding systems will also monitor and react to the heightening and lowering of our emotional state.

This interaction between our emotional state and bonding systems allows us to adjust our emotions using our bonding, but when our emotional state runs out of control this directly impacts our bonding systems too.

There is a pendulum below to demonstrate a woman's bonding equilibrium: -

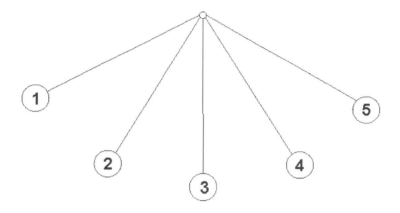

This pendulum has two sides and indicates a euphoric state of our emotional balance on the high side and a depressed emotional state on the low side.

Around the middle point is generally fine for us. But sexual pleasure is not always of the bonded variety and the pendulum can swing along with our emotional state. An example of this is a young female who has been raped and experienced violent sex and a violent orgasm. As her equilibrium point is not anchored it can shift dramatically to the low side around number two. Once her bonding has been set out of the normal range it is very difficult to bond in the normal way. Her sex life has been ruined; she needs heavy sexual stimulation to generate euphoria to lift the depression and also needs to use rough sex so she can reach her emotional high point to release her emotions as she orgasms.

She needs very active emotional management now because Mother Nature has moved her pendulum, sent her into a low emotional state which generates depression. She has also extended the range of her emotional highs to suit her alpha male (Stockholm Syndrome), and he was the rapist, so she doesn't want his attention any time soon and her natural bonding process has been compromised. Her orgasms will release and balance her emotions but the extended range of her emotional high point will be difficult to attain to orgasm properly and drain her emotions.

Why has Mother Nature moved her bonding to suit her alpha male you ask? Well we are monkeys and the females submit to the alpha male or leader of the troop. They naturally anchor their equilibrium point to him and orgasm for him so they breed successfully. For a woman this can be very damaging if the swing causes her equilibrium point to swing away from the centre. Bonding is still possible on the low side, but finding a male that can generate strong euphoria and behaves like a rapist is not easy. Just how do you tell a guy that you like really rough sex?

On the low side at point two I found women that enjoy a lot of sexual activity, rape victims, abused women, whores, women experimenting with BDSM and women that had been forced into that group because their breeding had faltered. They all needed to be struggle for one reason or another and faced difficult bonding issues. And as we have seen in the case of rape victims, when your equilibrium is not anchored it can slide ever lower or it can start to swing and you might need huge amounts of euphoria to reach your orgasms.

This group also have to contend with needing more extreme arousal to ignite their euphoria as time goes by to get their orgasms. They need to push their limits in order to get a state of euphoria and a strong orgasm to fully release their emotions when they suffered from increasing levels of depression, which can be mild, moderate or severe.

Women not only struggle on the low side but also find Mother Nature will try to stimulate them if they rise to the high side. Why does Mother Nature do this you may wonder? Well females need to be biologically lower than their males. They need to submit to orgasm and breed successfully. Monkeys simply cannot put the female higher than the male; it is the alpha male that is charge of breeding not the alpha female. When the female places herself above her male counterparts she naturally suppresses her bonding and her orgasms weaken. She just does not feel submissive towards those males anymore and her breeding has faltered. Also, rape victims that did not orgasm can become alpha females too, because they used their pride to suppress their breeding cycle.

Bonding on the high side at number four is now very difficult when her breeding cycle has been compromised in such a way. Mother Nature of course does not like this at all, she placed us on the planet with a few simple fundamental rules, organise security, eat and breed. So Mother Nature responds to alpha females on the high side with less sexual inhibition and a desire for sex in the euphoric emotional state.

When an alpha female encounters a rising pendulum cycle, because her bonding has been compromised she is forced into enter a hypomanic or manic phase where there is less sexual inhibition, and the manic episode becomes sexually invigorated as a high sex drive is generated to try and release and exhaust the higher emotional state. Where a woman has been suppressing her sex drive there can be weaker orgasms and that can makes it more difficult and the manic state will continue being sexually invigorated until her emotional high state is released and the pendulum swings back down again.

Mother Nature has resolved her faltering breeding cycle by turning her into a woman who is sexually invigorated and chasing orgasms. When her pendulum swings down, emotions do not always end up back in the perfect place and if she remains on the high side as alpha females can she can easily have her emotions rise again back towards another manic phase and enter another sexually invigorated cycle.

If her emotions swing all the way through the centre onto the low side she will enter a depression cycle and this is known as bipolar because she has entered a lethargic emotional state and a low sex drive state. On the low side at number two she will be forced to seek euphoria to climb back out of the depression cycle and heavy sexual stimulation can help her do that. She too will find her equilibrium point is not anchored on the low side and further lethargy will mean stronger depression and the orgasms harder to find without stronger and stronger arousal to start her euphoria and generate her orgasms.

Euphoria is directly linked to a higher sex drive and when we become elated during sex we feel this emotion being generated. Depression is directly linked to a lowering of our sexual state and a lowering of our sex drive and it is the opposite and balancing emotion for euphoria. The two emotions can never occur together, we will always be in a neutral state or a high emotion state generating euphoria or a low emotion state generating depression.

The bonding equilibrium directly relates to our emotional state which strengthens with strong bonding and stable emotions, whereas euphoria and depression relate directly to our sexual state but exists alongside our bonding equilibrium as the breeding cycle is used to help maintain our bonding.

However, euphoria and depression can be generated at any point on our bonding equilibrium which will dictate how much euphoria we will need to get to a point of an orgasm and how strong the orgasm will be when we get there. The stronger the orgasm we can generate the better our emotional release will be and the better our emotional state and bonding equilibrium will balance up after sexual activity for our bonding.

When we are already in a high emotional state it is harder for Mother Nature to use euphoria of course and orgasms are naturally weaker and balancing our emotion state becomes harder. Because euphoria indicates our sexual state we generate very high amounts during sexual activity and Mother Nature will then generate balancing amounts of depression to return us back to our current euphoric state after the sexual activity has concluded and we will adjust our bonding equilibrium to our new emotional state which will have lowered due to the emotional releases.

When our bonding equilibrium rises Mother Nature naturally raises our euphoric state to generate a higher sex drive until she reaches the manic episode where she uses strong sexual invigoration to initiate emotional releases and correct our bonding equilibrium. After sex has concluded the balancing emotion of depression is used to calm euphoria with a balancing emotional force and that is when the depression is generated, so in the orgasm chase depression is used to calm our emotions after our euphoria and sexual activity. Euphoria is a high emotion and depression it's balancing low emotion.

The lowering of our sexual state with depression also lowers the sex drive which happens naturally after sex and depression rebalances and calms our sexual emotions. A depression condition itself is caused by lowering the euphoric state and sex drive and when there is a negative euphoric state depression is the dominating emotion and condition. If we swing our emotions and generate a lowering of our emotional state and we lower our sex drive we can also generate depression, this can be born out and demonstrated with the following examples:-

1) The high levels of euphoria and sexual invigoration during a manic higher emotional state can trigger a rapid emotional heightening event and then a crash which causes a total drain of our emotional state and an excess of lowering the euphoric state and sex drive. When the manic phase is over we are left with the bonding equilibrium falling to the low side after the emotional drain. We enter a depressive state where there is also a low sex drive, which is what we know as bipolar. As there was an excess of emotional releases

our low emotional state causes lethargy and our euphoric state swings down into a depressive state.

2) Anorexic females are found in a very high state of euphoria, but when an anorexic female suppresses her violent sexual thoughts, lowers her sex drive and has ignored Mother Nature's sexual invigoration, the lowering of her sex drive lowers her euphoric state and that uses depression. When the euphoric state swings to a negative condition a depressive state is generated as the balancing emotion then takes precedence which is depression.

3) A subdued emotional state like grief can cause a subdued euphoric state and a subdued sex drive too. There are other examples of a subdued emotional state which can be initiated by personal problems or even some medications. This subdued emotional state produces depression when either the bonding equilibrium falls to the low side or the euphoric state lowers using depression and then the depression takes precedence.

This means that a bipolar condition can get an escalating depression condition if the bonding equilibrium continues to fall to the low side while the lethargy continues. Euphoria gets harder and harder to generate as the bonding equilibrium falls and if it cannot be halted the depression slide continues until eventually that slide can end up at very end of the pendulum swing and there is a totally depressive state.

Depression is simply the manifestation of a low sexual state and a low sex drive and is used by Mother Nature when she lowers our high sexual state and high sex drive after euphoria and our sexual activity or when we have a low emotional state and lower our euphoric state and sex drive ourselves. Suppressing our euphoria will always result in depression if euphoria falls into a negative state and then the depression dominates too.

What is now clear is that there is a euphoric state for the higher side of the bonding equilibrium and a depressive state for the lower side of the bonding equilibrium and that is where we experience those emotions. Mother Nature never gives us depression, if she generated excess depression in the euphoric cycle she would defeat the very aim of that euphoric state. If she generated an excess of depression in the depression cycle we would never be able to climb back out of the depression state.

Instead, it is us that governs how we manage our emotions and where our bonding equilibrium rests. If we ignore the manic sexual invigoration there is a good chance that suppressing the euphoric state will end up with depression. Equally, if we totally drain our emotional state with exhaustion and other lowering emotions and we become lethargic, we will lower into a depressive cycle and exist in a depressed state until we generate excitement, elation and euphoria again.

A smaller swing for the bipolar condition is referred to hypomanic (or bipolar II) where there is a smaller rise in the pendulum and this is less severe than the manic condition. It is found that there is less sexual inhibition here too but women that suppress their sex drive and euphoric state in bipolar I and bipolar II can also trigger depression. Two other bipolar cycles, the cyclothymic and bipolar related also swing their pendulum as in bipolar I and bipolar II.

Anxiety is most commonly associated with depression but can occur whenever we enter a state of emotional turmoil. The hypomanic and manic cycle, anorexic cycle, depression cycle and even a neutral state can all be accompanied by anxiety and it is a good indicator that our emotional balance has moved away from the centre and our bonding is in jeopardy. Anxiety is particularly pronounced when indicating isolation and vulnerability which does not sit well with our bonding systems.

Sexually invigorated women (whether through the manic cycle or the depression cycle) tend to have a strong desire to be used by males because of their lack of bonding and spanking is a common practice to start an alpha female's submission process which heightens the body for a stronger emotional release and generates good submission which can be seen as her vagina starts to get wet as she is spanked.

What we see here is the use of a higher emotional state being generated by using pain and then getting a stronger emotional release through her orgasm and of course that will work well. But, just like the rape victim, if we start to raise the threshold for our emotional highs there is a risk that Mother Nature will always expect us to reach that height with our orgasms so she can fully release our emotions. This type of extending the emotional range needs to be understood as it impacts other females too besides rape victims and pain enthusiasts, women that are abused or use stronger sexual stimulation like BDSM or women that use drugs can also change their emotional boundaries and make orgasms difficult to reach.

Of course sometimes it is difficult for women to start to chase orgasms in our society, but the women mostly need more encouragement to breed. They are perhaps women that simply failed to bond in the normal timely fashion and anchor their bonding to their alpha male. Once properly bonded women can enjoy sex in the way Mother Nature intended.

When our belief system is joined to our bonding equilibrium sexual activity can be enjoyed and the bonding equilibrium no longer swings around, sometimes needing ever more arousal to ignite our orgasms. That is when we have successfully bonded, in the centre of the pendulum.

As we have self-determination Alpha females do not always like to actively chase orgasms of course and I think it is common for some to turn to alcohol and cannabis to alleviate their conditions. Breeding females will often find their bonding looking after their children and bond with their children too. But holding down a relationship with their alpha male has its problems and I think a lot of relationships fail for alpha females because their bonding is not as strong as it should be with their alpha males who sense they are not as submissive as they should be.

When Alpha Females go Pride High

You will have noticed the pendulum can go still higher than the alpha female. This is seriously high at number five and is simply pride high, where Mother Nature is forced to takes extreme measures.

This is because the alpha female has now suppressed her bonding totally. Orgasms are incredibly weak or none existent here. A high intake of pride or very high emotions has caused the alpha female to further suppress her bonding until she has none and she sees herself as superior to virtually all of her male counterparts.

This condition is perhaps more common than you think as society elevates women to extremely high levels when they have a celebrity status. Often women found here are singers, actresses, models, performers and high academic achievers and their working environment is a huge drain on their emotional ability to keep themselves in a more humble place. Some alpha females with a manic episode will also sometimes start to chase highs with drugs and high adrenaline activities which simply push their pendulum higher. This can happen naturally to performers, and some like to use exhaustion to try and alleviate the situation by going to the gym or running.

Mother Nature does not allow a woman to totally suppress her breeding cycle like this; in effect the female has impeded her breeding cycle. Her punishment is very severe; she causes insecurity, eating disorders like anorexia so the female struggles to eat and she stops her periods and her breeding cycle as she maintains the pride high state. In effect Mother

Nature is slowly terminating the female such is her venom when her breeding cycle is stopped in this fashion and anorexia occurs more towards the extreme end of here punishments at the high end of the pendulum.

But Mother Nature still tries to repair the situation though; she also creates insecurity and violent sexual thoughts. The insecurity when you are a monkey will drive you to stay closer to the alpha males and the violent sexual thoughts are the solution to the condition.

Human females will often try to take control of something that is important in their life to combat these feelings and try to fight the trust and anxiety issues sometimes making themselves paranoid. Often these obsessions will be around their appearance which is linked to their breeding cycle and what they must do to make themselves sexually attractive. Such an obsession will simply set their belief system or worship bonding side without a valid bonding value for the bonding equilibrium and this will release the bonding equilibrium and allow their pendulum to swing more freely, exasperating the failed bonding condition still further.

In effect Mother Nature is now trying to enforce her breeding. She has given up on the bonding process for this female and wants her to chase her orgasms to introduce her back into the breeding cycle. Of course we have self-determination and females die here because some simply do not know what is wrong or what to do about it. I think history is littered with famous females that could not cope with this condition and ended up killing themselves here. Also, there is another issue in that females simply do not want to submit like a monkey in our society and famous people do not want to chase orgasms as it is not easy for them to do so.

When anorexia is joined by depression this turns into an even more serious condition because the low sex drive condition prevents her from easily accessing her weak orgasms to release and exhaust her high emotional state. Just like position one, long periods of arousal play can be used to ease the depression so that she can reach her orgasms and start to relieve the emotionally high condition.

Obsessions about eating can also trigger a bulimic condition (binging and purging food by laxatives or vomiting) and when there is depression, anorexia and bulimia these make up a deadly combination that it is almost impossible to cope with.

It is worth mentioning here that not all females have an emotional drive on their bonding equilibrium and when this happens our belief system becomes stronger and worship is invoked instead, brats (who love themselves) fall into this category, they are very single minded and very stubborn and use worship bonding instead.

When females go Pride High there can be two conditions created, one from the bonding equilibrium release and another from the belief system which is generated by obsession and impacts their worship bonding system. So when they go pride high but the worship bonding system is still working we can get depression, manic episodes, anorexia and anxiety. The frustration, cravings, self-harming and suicidal thoughts are generated when we have a worship bonding failure (or obsession failure) because worship is a life force emotion.

A partnership breakup can trigger both of these sets of conditions, but where there is an obsession and that belief system remains in tack only the bonding equilibrium will encounter difficulties causing depression, anxiety, manic episodes and anorexia.

As we see in anorexia obsessions are a very common condition and obsessions are driven by sustained emotional heightening as we will see later, so anorexia is an emotional high condition as I discovered in my relationships. It seems apparent the Mother Nature governs all of her higher bonding through emotional heightening and it appears that Mother Nature is attempting to create a narcissistic bonding here through sustained emotional heightening, importance, violent sexual thoughts and insecurity; and this is a route to bonding and narcissism.

What is actually happening here is that Mother Nature has initiated her drive for importance and fulfilment and that drive starts obsessional behaviour and it is clear that it is targeted at the bonding and breeding process, as Mother Nature would not target an obsession about clothes and appearance, which often happens.

What we should note here though is that fulfilment is very much a part of Mother Nature's importance processes.

Anorexia is a very complex condition that varies in severity considerably and women that suffer from the emotionally high condition will find that they are always prone to suffer that way. Given there are so many different intensities choosing the correct level of bonding can also be a matter of judgement.

Where there is only a mild condition and an obsession has not been triggered the Active Bonding process should be sufficient to relieve the pride levels and lower the bonding equilibrium and allow a successful bonding process to engage.

However, anorexia commonly triggers an obsession and what Mother Nature does here is to instigate subjugation and control with a compulsion and cravings. We will see later that this is a part of Mother Nature's importance and ideally would initiate narcissistic bonding but humans need something that they can control and then in turn, it controls them through an obsession.

Once this has happened we have to choose a more suitable method of bonding that can deal with an obsession and narcissism offers this. Narcissistic Bonding can be sufficient here to provide a high emotional drive and relieve the obsession naturally when the obsession is not too severe.

When anorexia is severe and a life threatening condition is encountered though, either through starvation or an obsession failure and becoming suicidal, an Extended Narcissistic Bonding (or Extreme Narcissistic Bonding) option is more appropriate. This is especially true when a bulimia condition has been triggered.

I will explain an obsession in detail so you can fully understand what is happening. When Mother Nature registers the emotional heightening she generates an importance for that event and it will be controlled because it is important. What we also see is that when we control something it naturally subjugates us to remain within the controlling force.

If we take a maximum situation like life and death we see maximum emotional heightening generating maximum importance and a maximum controlling force established over the process and then we are subjugated to take the best action to preserve our life. We call this the will to live.

If we take a more normal situation like going to the movies we have some anticipation generating the emotional heightening and that then generates the importance, a controlling force is established over the process to make us watch the movie and we are subjugated to remain seated throughout the movie. If the movie is poor the emotional heightening falls, the importance falls, our controlling force to watch the movie dwindles and the subjugation to remain seated ebbs away until we get up and leave.

Now if we take a situation where there is sustained emotional heightening and we generate sustained importance the controlling force is sustained too and the subjugation of the controlling force is sustained and we call that an obsession. So where the controlling force is clothes we are obsessional about clothes.

In anorexia when the controlling force is clothes there is no action taken against the bonding equilibrium pendulum because that is not the subject or element under control and subjugation. It remains free and able to swing and if anything the control over the bonding equilibrium pendulum diminishes further. The anorexic condition remains and even escalates.

However, In anorexia when the controlling force is breeding, as Mother Nature tries to press, the narcissistic obsession uses human bonding and that does take a controlling action against the bonding equilibrium pendulum because that is the subject under control. It is subjugated and under the control of the worship bonding system as a state of worship is generated.

Now we see how a narcissistic bonding can cure anorexia and other related bonding equilibrium issues too and why this obsession has to be maintained to keep it as an important factor in our lives. Our belief systems believe this to be important for our lives to have a purpose and when we try to stop the obsession we lose that belief and our importance, leaving us feeling frustrated, worthless and then suicidal.

Notice how Mother Nature can regulate and even generate an obsession without us even noticing and she is dictating where the importance in our lives should be. When the importance increases the controlling force increases and then the subjugation will also increase too. She ensures we maintain our importance to maintain our lives. We will see that narcissism is all about obsessional bonding and how Mother Nature can dictate this process and use it to control us.

Here again it is also common for females to try and alleviate their bonding equilibrium conditions through drugs and alcohol. Cannabis is a favourite for the women here who find they are able to eat again and alcohol can become a compulsive habit too.

In an extreme situation a woman who is pride high can also make use of emotional heightening to help her generate a stronger orgasm and emotional release, but that as we have seen, also has issues of its own when extreme emotional releases are used with our emotions. Using this process can subsequently make our emotions more difficult to manage and we should note that anorexia is a bonding failure and this would only be a temporary solution and could be harmful to regulating the bonding equilibrium emotional balance.

Female Narcissists

Narcissists are not always appreciated and they are often referred to as brats, but they are higher ranking females that have self-importance and they cannot be expected to answer to lower ranking males. Some believe these females are out of control and totally ungovernable. What happens though is they are allowed to keep their self-importance and high standing in that they are detached from their bonding equilibrium system.

A female narcissist will not suffer from becoming pride high or a bipolar condition because there is no emotional drive on her bonding equilibrium, effectively she does not have a bonding equilibrium and she does not suffer from depression, manic episodes, anorexia and anxiety, because she has bonded with herself using her worship bonding system. Only a worship bonding failure will disrupt her bonding and then she will suffer from frustration, self-harming, feeling worthless and suicidal thoughts with a termination of her worship bonding and a belief system failure and this substantial emotional trauma is encountered because of her strong worship dependency.

Their bonding is completed by worship alone as they have their worship bonding set to themselves and only worshiping their partner can they modify that bonding. Once they worship their partner they are bought under their partner's governance and their bonding and breeding cycle is secured.

It would appear society can generate as many brats (or narcissists) as it wishes but they are driven to find males they can worship and if they attempt to bond without being able to worship their partner, when they do not remain aloof and do not worship they suffer a belief system failure and this will happen if their alpha male does not accept their worship. A worship bonding failure leads them to become suicidal and their bonding is ruined. A brat should only bond once because it is so difficult for someone who is aloof to find another partner to worship and the worship failure is difficult to fight and eventually impossible to fight if they turn suicidal.

It would seem that the number of brats are naturally restricted and kept in balance with the number of males that can be worshipped and the excess will often become suicidal. Society can create huge numbers of brats but Mother Nature simply removes the ones who do not fit with society. I find this achievement by Mother Nature absolutely astounding. There is a case to argue that these brats are some sort of human queen and they are definitely engineered to be so.

Brats are probably created at a very early age when they obsess about their own self-importance and this behaviour is sometimes noticed in monkey's where the queens daughter is kept away from the other younger monkeys and made to be more important.

Entering events like pageants will have a high risk to a young girl in this respect, as will any competitive type activity where they can generate a high self-esteem. School is also used to set our belief system in life and the head girl is also held in high esteem and will be at risk of becoming a brat. Our home life too sets our belief system, very young children may start to escalate their self-importance by using temper tantrums which may be an early indicator that a self-importance obsession is being formed and girls who are called princess or treated like a princess may also end up as a brat and parents will often encourage and reward high achievement and a high standing.

Because brats cannot bond easily they may be forced to remain single, attempt an unsuitable bonding or they may be drawn to worship high ranking males like pop stars when they are younger which are all undesirable.

High achieving girls are encouraged more and more in our society and if we don't understand how Mother Nature works they are in for a torrid time if they cannot resolve their bonding later on in life. Brats can also accept worship as a form of bonding, but they must always give themselves by worship to their alpha male and ideally that will be a narcissistic male who will accept a worshipping female.

These are usually exceptionally talented women and they have the natural ability to take a male who has had a worship bonding failure and force the male to worship them. Females who take submissive males are called a Mistress in BDSM.

On occasion it is possible to get a hybrid female who is a brat who also has a small bonding equilibrium and I have met such a woman, she had completed a BDSM test (bdsmtest.org) and been provided with character analysis. The traits that had been graded included a high score for being a brat. When I discovered her personality it was true that she had had a small amount of depression when she was younger but it was clear that her brat side was the dominant side and biologically her emotional drive was for a brat too.

The fact that we can create brats at a later age after the bonding equilibrium has started to form is concerning in itself. Brats have major problems in life due to their worship bonding biology and we will see that although it is a good idea for Mother Nature to be able to create female leaders at a later stage in life, girls that generate the self-important persona and worship bonding traits in our normal society life will often struggle their entire lives.

Of course the purity of a brat is not all that important here, just the fact that they have become a brat and adopted that biology. Brats do not see themselves as submissive towards males and they only submit to one male, that is their alpha male. Their biology is very different in that when their partner degrades them (sexually or otherwise) they are forced into worship to resolve their bonding. And the more severely they are degraded the more fiercely they must worship. They need to feel the power of their narcissistic partner to worship successfully.

This side of their bonding is critical to them because if they set their worship bonding to their partner and then they are then denied their worship, their bonding starts to fail and they encounter a worship bonding failure. They need to include worship bonding in their relationship such as that later described in Narcissistic Bonding section where worship bonding is dealt with.

What we actually see here though is Mother Nature's bonding by obsession. When importance is raised to high levels it drives an obsession and here self-importance drives obsessional behaviour to establish self-importance. This obsession then impacts the bonding equilibrium in that it is a human bonding and the bonding equilibrium is then controlled and subjugated and is no longer active.

This is quite a feat by Mother Nature as she allows importance to establish high ranking females and removes the restriction of a bonding equilibrium. Brats are also the absolute proof that narcissistic bonding always controls and subjugates the equilibrium bonding system.

As this type of bonding is driven by obsession the bonding process with a narcissistic male must also be achieved by emotional heightening and importance so that she can drive a new obsession and bond successfully. Once obsessional bonding has been established bonding must always be maintained by obsessional bonding as we will see.

Male Narcissists

Male narcissists are often seen as very dominant and they are leaders. They are the King or Commander in Chief or our Tribal Chief. They are used to leading and ruling but do not always fit easily into our society if they are not in such a lofty position because they can exaggerate and degrade people to improve their high standing and these are the self-important males.

Of course bonding with such a powerful high standing female is not a simple thing to do. What narcissists demonstrate though is that when they degrade their partners they can illicit worship and for a female narcissist this is ideal. She is subjugated by her male dominant partner and this battle can often be intense.

There is emotional heightening as he drives importance and then this initiates control and subjugates her and he sets her worship bonding. This will establish a bonding obsession and she will become bonded to him. She too sustains his emotional heightening and drives his importance while he is controlling and subjugating her and this too establishes control and subjugation and sets his worship bonding to her by a bonding obsession too.

Notice how importance, control and subjugation are used here and this is very much a part of narcissism. A male narcissist will always strive to control and promote his high standing and importance. That is also how our worship bonding systems work, they allow control and subjugation to be initiated and followed while we observe our state of worship.

However, although many believe that narcissism is all about control that is not the full story. It is Mother Nature's importance for our belief systems and their maintenance, just like we saw self-importance creating a female narcissist here self-importance creates a male narcissist. What they do then is generate importance by emotional heightening for each other so their bonding establishes firm values in their belief systems and this uses Mother Nature's obsessional bonding.

Perhaps such an event is only what you would expect Mother Nature to achieve in her amazing biological world. Her bonding pinnacle is a true work of art and this is the highest level of bonding we can achieve and it is based on importance, control and subjugation and will often be the tools they use to establish importance for their high standing.

Not only can they do this for themselves but they can do it to others too and that is where control and subjugation is often seen and referred to as narcissism. But what we can see here is Mother Nature's ability to both recognise importance in humans and support that importance but also Mother Nature's ability create humans that are importance experts and can lead by delivering that importance to others.

However, women I have met with find this very disturbing if they are not narcissists themselves as the degrading appears to be abuse. A narcissist male will insist he is worshipped by his partner and will always demonstrate his superiority.

This can lead to some unusual acts, if he is defeated by a device like a phone for example; as he cannot be seen to fail he is likely to simply destroy the phone to reassert his high standing and authority. Again, if he is seen to fail in front of his partner he is likely to abuse her to show his authority and maintain his high standing and so his partners worship.

Where a female partner is not a narcissist and not expecting to be abused this relationship can be one of turmoil. They can regularly fight and the abuse can erupt into violence. Sadly these relationships can continue in a state of chaos for many years and because they have set their worship bonding, established importance and they cannot easily separate.

From women I have met this is a huge problem if they later decide to split from their partners to escape from this abuse as they suffer a worship bonding failure and then they are diagnosed with PTSD (post-traumatic stress disorder). This is because the emotional heightening and importance drives a bonding obsession and an obsession failure can be devastating.

It seems that just like a female narcissist cannot bond with a male she cannot worship and establish a bonding obsession with and needs a male narcissist, an ordinary woman that does not need worship bonding cannot feel comfortable with the narcissistic abuse that joins the partnership in a worship bonding. They then find it difficult to separate from such a partnership that has used a bonding obsession and often get abused for many years before they decide to leave.

Abuse is very subjective in itself of course and as we see here one person's abuse is another person's nectar. But abuse in reality is a forced situation where one person expressly imposes their will on another person that does not wish that to happen. In the case of narcissistic bonding by narcissists they both need this to happen and you cannot really argue with Mother Nature.

This creates quite a complexity in our bonding, but narcissistic bonding reveals how we can use worship bonding ourselves to set our worship bonding with partners. Narcissistic bonding is the very pinnacle of our bonding because it uses a bonding obsession and worship is our highest level of bonding and it is set by emotional heightening that establishes importance within our belief systems.

As society changes we are moving away from deliberate abuse and subjugation and as we will see later there are other ways to set our worship bonding, establish a bonding obsession and take advantage of narcissism without abuse in Narcissistic Bonding.

We will also see how an obsession sets our worship bonding and that we are described as having a compulsion and that we can see the same cravings in an obsession break down as we see in narcissistic bonding failure. These cravings cause subjugation and the need to be controlled to re-establish our worship bonding and repair the emotional importance in our belief systems.

Bonding Ruination

This is where our bonding has reached severe difficulties and extreme techniques are sometimes deployed. This may include women with a major depression condition and she needs strong sexual stimulation to ease the depression and find her orgasms. She may also of had a worship bonding failure and becoming suicidal and also needing a strong emotional release to ease her cravings. Equally a pride high condition may have become too difficult to manage and her orgasms too weak to generate an effective emotional release.

As females enter ruination their sex drive is so low they pursue all sorts of extreme arousal techniques to reach their orgasms and relieve their failed bonding condition. I will not go into all the types of humiliation and degrading techniques used here but you can see it on the BDSM web sites (an overlapping abbreviation of Bondage and Discipline (BD), Dominance and Submission (DS), Sadism and Masochism (SM). Some women also like pain to heighten the body before they submit to increase the intensity of the orgasm here, so flogging and canning can be used too. Other techniques like breathe control are also used and figging can provide good submission too.

These are desperate times for the woman and some will spend a couple of hours doing arousal role play like pet play first. Dressing up as say a kitten, whiskers drawn on the face, ears on the head, a collar and leash and even a butt plug tail and cat litter allow her to increase her humiliation and sexually stimulate herself in front of her alpha male before they engage in sex itself. This prolonged arousal slowly eases the depression and relieves pride as she increases her arousal and she becomes sexually stimulated and can manage to orgasm again.

There are other forms of submission that can help too; a woman on all fours can have her head held to the floor sideways on so she can see her alpha male and this is widely used in the animal kingdom. Humans can also serve on their knees, which is also a good submissive position. Bondage is also popular to generate total submission and forcing a woman to beg has the same effect.

Why do women use submission and go to such extreme lengths you may wonder? The route of this lies in our bonding processes and especially narcissism. A narcissist male who believes he is a true leader and subjugates his partners and followers to invoke worship in our bonding. He is the tribal leader, the commander in chief, the one that commands our respect. Just as Mother Nature's narcissism uses subjugation for bonding other females can heighten their emotional state using submission.

When ruination includes a worship bonding failure the only remaining solution is to introduce narcissism our most powerful bonding. Such is the power of narcissism it can set a woman's bonding equilibrium to her alpha male when she worships him.

When Mother Nature recognises that an acute bonding failure has occurred because of a narcissistic bonding failure she introduces frustration, sexual cravings and worthlessness which makes a woman feel suicidal.

There are some interesting views on Extreme Narcissistic Bonding. Some women believe that they do not need to love and bond in Extreme Narcissistic Bonding and that the ruination should just continue and their limits continue to be pushed. There are alpha males (Masters) that do not believe in anything other than that the ruination should continue and the limits continued to be pushed. And there are females that reject their current partners because their bonding obsession has failed because they are the ones that have ruined them, even if they are married partners. Brats especially are found here due to their dependency on worship bonding and not being able to find a partner they can successfully worship and drive their obsessional bonding.

What Mother Nature is offering here are the riches that can be found in worship or an obsessional bonding, a total union of worship where they become one with their alpha male and he looks after all of their needs and then both benefit from the uplift of this relationship as they are refreshed in their life and they live as one.

This symbiotic style of bonding stabilises a deteriorating life as the women is granted Mother Nature's total happiness, which she gives with her total bonding, total humiliation, total submission and total love. This can also provide a rejuvenating quality for her too.

Brats need to maintain their belief system which is not to submit, they are of a high standing and aloof and this makes submission and their orgasms a lot different. They only way that a brat can submit is to invoke the most powerful of her emotions worship and use her bonding obsession, which can subdue their high standing belief system while she submits with worship.

Narcissistic bonding can be very difficult if they choose a partner that is not a narcissist because she may not get sufficient emotional heightening and importance to allow her to bond with her partner and in that event she will remain unbound and vulnerable to chase bonding elsewhere, like idolising pop stars or even stalking.

There is another possible outcome here too in that she may feel she needs to love her partner and starts to engage her worship bonding systems by obsession when she gets married to him. It is very easy for a brat to fall into this trap as she will be strongly driven to love her partner and if an obsession occurs she might then struggle to maintain that obsession over her lifetime if her male partner is not a narcissist.

It is common for brats to find the pressures of our modern day lifestyle too much to keep such an obsession going for her partner and when that obsession starts to ebb she incurs a narcissistic bonding failure. Brats that suffer such a failure will often fight it for many years by using orgasms to relieve their frustration and their cravings.

Also, she may find that her partner heightened her emotions sufficiently to set her worship bonding when they got married but as her partner is not a narcissist they simply do not understand a worshipping female so they do not know how to look after their bonding and heighten them sufficiently to maintain their importance and bonding obsession and this will eventually lead to a narcissistic bonding failure.

Brats will often try to maintain their orgasms and will often become submissives and get a Master to help them generate their orgasms which they find therapeutic when they are engaged in ruination, but if they do not worship their Master they do not get bonding fulfilment and they just continue the orgasm chase until their cravings overwhelm them and they are struggling with suicidal thoughts and some move to resolve this condition in Extreme Narcissistic Bonding.

Dealing with our worship bonding systems can be difficult in a modern society and an area in which celebrities suffer is the impact of a sort of reverse crush, they can obsess about their fans and set there worship bonding by obsession. If there is no valid bonding value for their bonding equilibrium here the bonding equilibrium will then release. This is naturally combined with a huge infusion of pride and the seeds to pride high are sewn. Many celebrities end up as bipolar because they do not understand what obsessing over their fans can do to them.

Performers and singers are exposed to high levels of hysteria and often fall into this trap too, their pendulum releases and they swell on the infusion of pride, and if they obsess about their fans they will set their worship bonding too.

When they retire, move their lives on and move away from their fans, they too can find they have to contend with a worship bonding failure and PTSD, as well as a bipolar condition.

The conditions encountered here are often referred to as BPD or Borderline Personality Disorder, and this is evolving for the statistics, but in the US it is put at between 1.6% and 2.7% of the adult population (245m) so perhaps around 2% will be roughly five million people. Also the figures suggest the women account for between 75% and 90% of the patients diagnosed, so 80% will give you approximately four million women with bonding difficulties and potentially entering ruination. Of course for the brats this will always be ruination and it is thought that around 83% of the BPD sufferers also get depression. That indicates that 17% of these sufferers who do not get depression will be brats and the US has well over 600,000 adult women brats currently in ruination.

Active Bonding

Mother Nature does allow you to both have a sexually active life and bond successfully when you have emotional problems but there needs to be a little work around the bonding equilibrium management. The training programme I used with my partners was very effective at anchoring the woman's equilibrium point and providing enhanced sexual stimulation and strong orgasms for a good emotional balance.

Establishing the correct level of sexual play for arousal and the sexual euphoria itself are fundamental to good orgasms and a happy life. This introduction provides a sound foundation to securing the bonding equilibrium balance with a partner and anchoring it to him. He can then successfully help manage the equilibrium going forward.

I used this process to go to breast orgasms, edging without touching and orgasms without touching and it can be even done with an online messaging system.

I discovered that peeing and edging are incredibly good forms of sexual play which can also impact the bonding equilibrium balance and help anchor the bonding equilibrium to the centre of the pendulum and prevent the emotional swings that are present in emotional trauma and bonding disruption.

My female partners peed for me every day to refresh their emotional connection with me, the toilet will do and they just sent me a picture on a messaging system. Peeing for someone forces them to give themselves and helps the belief system accept the bonding process; it relieves pride, generates arousal and refreshes the bonding equilibrium and bonding. It was incredibly good for them and initiated effective bonding and strong orgasms.

My partners also edged for me every day, that is rubbing their clitoris until they nearly cum, then pausing and rubbing a little more until their clitoris starts to throb a little and then stop. They soon learnt to enjoy a swollen clitoris for their guy.

If edging is difficult for you, you can try a little toothpaste on your clitoris or a clitoris stimulation cream to really activate your clitoris. Then simply tell your partner when an edge has completed for him, to involve him more in your enhanced sex life.

To increase the sexual euphoria for my partner's orgasms I asked her to spread her pussy lips and send me a picture to show me how wet she is for me. Whether chatting or being physical you can then enjoy a good strong orgasm.

To include breasts in the edging process, once you enjoy edging with your clitoris you simply start to close your legs and squeeze your throbbing clitoris between them. Then learn how to continue the edge massaging your breasts and squeezing your nipples.

Once you can edge with your breasts I like to move to breast orgasms, where you stimulate your clitoris with normal edging and then hold your legs tightly closed whilst you massage your breasts and squeeze your nipples and then orgasm for your guy. He should enjoy the fact that you can do this for him.

Now you can edge with both your clitoris and breasts you can edge without touching. All you have to do is close your legs and rock on your hips gently; you can feel your clitoris swell and start to throb as your nipples start to tingle too. You can actually do this anywhere, more than once a day if you wish, while you are chatting with your guy and tell him what you are doing for him and how you feel him inside you.

I found that I could make my partners clitoris swell by just chatting to her and get her to start edging anytime I wanted, and she loved it. Such was the strength of the arousal I could even bring her to orgasm by just chatting to her and with no touching at all. My partner, a woman who was a manic depressive (bipolar) that had attempted suicide several times was loving life now. This type of bonding had stabilised my partner's bonding equilibrium to help form the relationship and then I was able to create a normal loving relationship.

The thing that stood out here was my partner's effectively dead clitoris was impacting her capability to get a good sexual stimulation and a good sex drive. She had been told not to touch down there when she was young girl and that she was a dirty girl when she did that. When this persisted she was taken to a psychologist who helped break the habit and stopped her touching her clitoris and no doubt instilled guilt in her.

A woman's clitoris is incredibly important to generate her sexual spark and her emotional wellbeing. Once we used a clitoris stimulating cream for ten days to establish her edging her clitoris was active again and swelling for me naturally. By massaging her breasts while she held her throbbing clitoris tightly between her legs and stimulated her breasts and nipples aggressively to continue the edge enabled her to do breast orgasms for me another ten days later and ten days later she was edging without touching. The nice thing about the breast orgasms and edging without touching was they were still easy to do on my partner's period. The two month relationship had seen her move from that of emotional turmoil to a vibrant and happy woman.

What we see here is that her clitoris was used to create a strong sexual stimulation and sex drive which eased the depression and was combined with peeing which enabled a strong bond to be established. This was powerful enough to move her pendulum back to the centre and hold it there where she could orgasm successfully again. She was so emotionally responsive she could orgasm after edging without touching by just sexual chat alone and she was a truly amazing woman.

A key difference here is that worship was not engaged to create a belief system. In fact, my partner did not believe any of this would work. Instead the belief system was built gradually exploring, experiencing and discovering the things that worked. That instilled a greater belief in her partner, and more of a desire to go further. The belief was built and proven without worship being used at all and that of course is how we build and learn to love too.

Using chat for emotional management is a skill in itself of course and getting the desired results might take some practice. I found that when I guided orgasms it was better to get my partner to edge first and get her clitoris throbbing for me so she could feel me inside her. Establishing a strong connection is important and she needs to know she is doing this for me. Whilst she becomes fully aroused I could look at her body and describe what her body was doing for me, her throbbing clitoris, erect nipples and running pussy juices and get her to generate strong emotions by doing things for me.

To increase the emotional intensity she always had to ask for permission to orgasm and I always told her I expected her biggest orgasm for me before allowing her to do so. This process ensured a strong healthy orgasm that enabled her to fully exhausted her emotions and also get a strong sense of enjoyment and satisfaction while we were engaged in the sexual activities.

Notice that here a woman can use an act of submission to increases her euphoric state and heighten her emotional state leading to a stronger orgasm by simply asking for permission to orgasm.

Another woman I met suffered from high levels of anxiety, but her bonding equilibrium seemed quite normally balanced apart from some depression a few years previously. Instead her partner bonding had led to bad experiences and this made bonding difficult for her, even when she was married she did not get sexual fulfilment and would let her husband use her vagina and then retire to the bathroom to finish off her orgasm using her clitoris.

These emotional problems had led to poor bonding and partners leaving her, with her vagina not functioning normally and generating her orgasms she was not emotionally fulfilled and low in confidence with her partners. She felt like she would simply get used and partners would always move on, she was a victim and waiting for the next person to arrive and leave.

This had created high levels of anxiety for her and uncertainty and nervousness with men. As often with anxiety she had poor sleep patterns, sometimes waking up during the night several times and other times only being able to get a couple of hours sleep, sometimes feeling exhausted and needing to retire early because of her anxious state. Her emotions were unstable too, sometimes crying while we were chatting, although she felt at ease with me. She had increased her problems by coming to a foreign country to work and that had also increased her sense of isolation and vulnerability.

She loved feeling a swollen clitoris and edging for me and it gave her a lot of pleasure. We chatted for long periods and she was desperate to feel her bonding settle and gain emotional stability. She had sought out a partner online because she did not feel able to settle normally in a relationship and needed a male partner to help guide her and making sure she was sexually fulfilled and emotionally complete.

She was in her mid-forties and had developed the first signs of menopause and was a little shocked. I suspect that menopause had triggered a little early because she had not been using her vagina and relying on her clitoris for her orgasms and that had caused Mother Nature to act earlier than she might have done.

She liked an active bonding process because she did not have emotional stability and she needed what active bonding and a partner could give to her, bringing her stability by joining more effectively with a partner that would guide her and bring back her confidence and allow her to complete her bonding process.

What is also clear with active bonding is that when a woman exposes her peeing activity she naturally generates anxiousness as she would crouching down in the long grass before civilisation and exposing herself to a potential attack by predators. When instead this is done with a partner an emotional swing is generated and the initial anxiousness is then replaced by trust and security, as these emotions take precedence anxiety is quelled naturally. Of course, when a partnership generates trust and security this is a natural basis for love and this then strengthens the love in the relationship.

My experiences with anxiety always seems to show emotional instability and poor bonding but not always with a swinging bonding equilibrium, although anxiety generally accompanies other conditions like depression or anorexia it can occur anytime there is emotional instability.

The peeing activities here were also effective at relieving pride when the bonding equilibrium had started to climb and alleviating this condition allowed the bonding equilibrium to lower again. This showed that the active bonding process is also suitable for milder anorexia where an obsession has not been triggered. Here again the edging helped generate the sexual stimulation and arousal too.

Women did find the peeing activity strange at first but soon found out this was also fun and enjoyed exposing themselves to me, so much so that they would often have a swollen clitoris for me whilst they were peeing for me. I found the thought of my partner feeling me so strongly whilst they were peeing for me quite a turn on too.

I found that the active bonding process was extremely effective at dealing with all of the conditions related to the bonding equilibrium, where depression was counteracted by the good use of an arousal process which in turn helped stimulate an active sex life. Anxiety, bipolar and anorexia were all helped by creating an emotional swing by peeing for me and generating a strong sense of trust and security and alleviating pride where necessary.

Of course when we use partnership bonding we need to consider both sides of the coin and when we use active bonding with emotional management techniques the male too can benefit from stronger bonding in a similar fashion.

So the female should encourage regular erections from her partner and edging too can be very stimulating for him. She can hold his penis as he takes a pee (let him start first to avoid an erection) and increase their partnership bonding. Remember his penis belongs to you and you must always govern it.

Using such a strong bonding process as this active bonding can be bought down to just a few minutes a day and I discovered that a pee and an edge can also be very pleasurable with your partner and it was amazing how it improved the bonding equilibrium and provided good emotional health.

When using such an active bonding process it is important not to let external influences impact the bonding and porn should be avoided or watched together. Partnerships also have to consider how to manage their sex drives and when one of them is not feeling sexy here it is important that all masturbation is handled within the partnership with the other partner present or helping so the masturbation does not become a temptation that is outside of the bonded partnership.

The important thing to notice here is that we do not use subjugation or control to enforce the bonding process and the partners can maintain a more balanced relationship.

Narcissistic Bonding

The nice thing about narcissistic bonding is that you don't need to use subjugation and control in an abusive way to complete narcissistic bonding; you can use submission instead and allow your partner to use emotional management techniques. This means that you do not need a narcissistic partner to set your worship bonding and you can use emotional heightening and importance instead when it is combined with control elements and subjugation to drive Mother Nature's bonding obsession.

Emotional heightening can be very enjoyable too of course and it can deal with sexual cravings and there is help available for those with a worship bonding failure (PTSD). Some women may already be trying to resolve self-harming issues, suicidal thoughts and a feeling of worthlessness as the cravings grow and consume their lives and want to use narcissistic bonding to resolve these conditions.

Other complex conditions that have resulted in obsessions that are undesirable can also be tackled here by using emotional heightening, importance and sexual pleasure to replace the obsession and secure their worship bonding system through a bonding obsession.

What we will see here is that we can use emotional heightening to generate Mother Nature's importance for our belief systems and that will provide us with a strong purpose in life, it instigates a controlling force and subjugation to facilitate our bonding. It can relieve a belief system failure, the cravings and the feelings of worthlessness that are part of such an event. Generating fulfilment through emotional heightening and stronger emotional releases allows Mother Nature's importance processes to engage and establish a strong purpose in their belief systems and secure their worship bonding system.

A successful therapy here is to introduce porn movies and to watch these regularly as they increase in intensity to match a woman's cravings. This therapy helps a woman normalise her feelings and accept her cravings as a normal emotional in life. As you would expect these movies increase in intensity until they reach BDSM movies where these become favourites. Of course there is a reason for that, the BDSM practices are very much in line with what a woman needs to satisfy her carvings and emotional needs.

This therapy of course will end up with a much greater reach, because when the woman normalises her thoughts about BDSM she will also want this in her sex life. If her partner is involved in the process he may find the more intense sexual activity very stimulating too and the pair may happily adopt this activity into their normal sex life. This greater intensity allows the woman to complete her obsession that has been triggered by Mother Nature's cravings and once Mother Nature's cravings are satisfied her worship bonding is set and her emotional state can be back in harmony again.

Of course if a woman does not have a partner this therapy will also encourage her to seek a more dominant male who will join with her in a more intense sexual way and enjoy a more extreme sex life. Such a man will be able to look after her emotional needs more completely and the ability to satisfy her cravings or resolve her obsession is absolutely essential to her.

Some popular practices here are bondage where a woman can be tied up and her erogenous zones stimulated until she reaches a very high state of sexual excitement and she cannot stop these emotions running to extreme intensities because she is bound and at the mercy of her partner.

Another approach that can generate extremely high intensities is sensory deprivation, where a woman's sight and hearing are blocked by masks and ear muffs. She is left to lie quietly for a period of time that might be 20 minutes or an hour or two and her body adjusts to the loss of her senses by increasing the sensitivity of her other senses. It is claimed that her sense of feel can be increased 100 times by this technique. Once in this state the touch of a feather can feel like that of a knife and intense pleasure enjoyed as her erogenous zones are teased and her emotions run high with such intense sexual pleasure.

Other techniques that are used are extremely powerful for bonding too and where a woman has to pee in front of her guy or has to suck cock for a period of time these acts have a profound impact on their bonding and create a powerful bond between the lovers.

Of course, not only is narcissistic bonding used to repair a worship bonding failure or obsessional dependency but for brats it is essential that they use these and other techniques to avoid an abusive relationship or a worship bonding failure. If they fail to establish a narcissistic bonding relationship their bonding can eventually fail, but here there are techniques that she can use to secure her narcissistic bonding needs.

The nice thing about using sexual heightening for brats is that they do not need a narcissistic partner and can avoid a worship bonding failure which will normally end up with them leaving their partner in a desperate attempt to resolve their cravings and failed obsessional bonding state. Here they can appreciate cock sucking as control and subjugation and bondage as a controlling force as they maintain a heightened state and this can be very pleasurable for both partners. This process will often be referred to as degrading for narcissists.

Narcissistic bonding is our pinnacle in bonding and it is also so powerful that women can resolve a worship bonding failures and can also resolve depression, bipolar, anorexia, self-harming, suicidal, bulimia and other obsessive conditions if a strong bond can be established and maintained by a bonding obsession. As we have seen a bonding obsession controls and subjugates the bonding equilibrium and all of the related conditions.

It is also important to recognise that when we are dealing with a worship bonding failure or obsessional behaviour or an obsession failure and suicidal thoughts we need to maintain a strong emotional drive to facilitate the bonding obsession and this can be achieved by daily activities.

Just like the Active Bonding process used daily activities, here we can also use them to generate a strong emotional commitment and facilitate an obsession by edging daily, a daily peeing activity and 10 minutes cock sucking each day too. Here we are using similar activities but we are using emotional heightening and importance with degrading to achieve our worship bonding because we are introducing subjugation and control. Guys may find this approach strange but they can soon learn to adapt and enjoy these activities too.

Clearly judging how much of an emotional drive is required to relieve an obsession or obsession failure will depend on each individual's needs, for example a younger woman may find this approach easily accommodates her needs but an older woman may need a higher level of intensity because of her life experiences. As additional tasks I found that Ben Wa Balls, body writing and a no panty day were all a lot of fun too.

All that happened here is we did what Mother Nature wanted instead of listening to all sorts of society inhibitions. This narcissistic bonding will work in most instances but where the cravings are extreme and a much more severe regime is needed to put the cravings at ease and an extreme approach to Narcissistic Bonding that uses these techniques 24/7 to normalise the cravings and extreme sexual activity is a used in Extreme Narcissistic Bonding.

There, where lives are in jeopardy due to extreme medical conditions such as attempting suicidal, anorexia with depression and bulimia can be tackled. In Extreme Narcissistic Bonding death can be averted and a content and happy life introduced as a woman's cravings are fulfilled and her worship bonding harmonised again.

Extreme Narcissistic Bonding

Here Mother Nature will tackle women who are facing death and repair their bonding system failures.

The concept of extreme narcissistic bonding is not very well understood and not widely used but some people are prepared to go to extreme lengths so they can live, and extreme narcissistic bonding is about saving the lives of people who are dying because of bonding failures.

Extreme Narcissistic Bonding simply extends narcissistic bonding into a 24/7 environment where extreme cravings can be normalised and then met. This especially applies to women that are suicidal and may have already attempted suicide, this is a choice that can be made, to be looked after in a state of total worship where total happiness and a repair of their worship bonding is possible. An uplift in their general health can also be found here.

What will happen here is that a belief system failure will be resolved by introducing Mother Nature's importance to such a level it will be all consuming and dominate their lives and repair their belief systems. This will in turn mean that they will only see one important purpose in life and it will provide them will all of the emotional heightening they need to stay alive. If sex is already the controlling force the male only needs to supply the emotional heightening and generate the importance for the narcissistic obsession to take hold. If sex is not the obsessional force here he needs to introduce sex to make that the controlling force.

Women that end up in extreme narcissistic bonding are often those that have no partners as their health deteriorates or perhaps those that leave their partners because they know they cannot satisfy their cravings in their current relationship. Without a partner to look after their cravings they turn to males that specialise in looking after women with these cravings, Masters from the world of BDSM.

These males are still a little amateurish because there is little formal training and there is so little understood about extreme narcissistic bonding, but a willingness to satisfy their cravings and allow them to enter a state of worship will form a solid basis to looking after a woman when she enters an extreme narcissistic bonding relationship.

Mother Nature generates a desire to serve, a need to be possessed and held in captivity. Typically, there is a strong need to be held in chains or caged close to her alpha male. This is a real need and requires micro management by the Master. Brats are the ones most likely to incur a narcissistic bonding failure because they have not been able to serve and worship in their relationship, when they have a greater dependency on worship in their bonding. What we are seeing here are cravings that need to be controlled by a narcissistic bonding obsession.

What is happening here is purely down to the way Mother Nature handles our failed bonding condition and a craving to re-instate it is generated. The women I have chatted with often find this hard to come to terms with and find it difficult to talk about, they are craving what are often extreme sexual acts and it is important to remember that it is the woman that drives the need for extreme narcissistic bonding and not the man, she needs someone to look after her now.

Although Mother Nature is now going to create a bond herself through a bonding obsession it does not happen in all cases, where the woman only wants ruination to continue and does not want to give herself or the Master only wants ruination and does not foster her need for possession, bonding cannot happen properly.

Bonding needs a little encouragement and then it will happen. The woman needs to be helped to accept her total submission. She has no rules; she is simply guided by her partner who uses emotional heightening and importance to facilitate a sexual obsession.

A woman with a bonding equilibrium may have a severe bipolar condition that cannot be managed or perhaps anorexia with depression and perhaps bulimia as well which will have made eating difficult and she may have sustained organ damage due to this, if she also has had a worship bonding failure she may have incurred nervous system damage and also be suicidal. These are serious medical conditions and women should avoid entering extreme narcissistic bonding if they can act sooner.

When the bonding equilibrium has swung to an extreme position arousal is vital to ignite her sexual stimulation and her orgasms again and get her emotional balance heading back towards the centre especially if depression is involved and there is a low sex drive causing emotional issues.

When you consider the combination of anorexia, depression and bulimia which can be deadly, extreme narcissistic bonding may be Mother Nature's only option to find a remedy for that. Indeed, any worship bonding failure or obsession or obsession failure or anorexic condition that has become life threatening has reached a state that makes extreme narcissistic bonding a wise cause of action and extreme narcissistic bonding can resolve all of the issues for the bonding equilibrium and the worship bonding system because it is the pinnacle in our bonding and it can dominate our bonding needs and sustain them in a bonding obsession.

The cravings will be slightly different in each case especially where there has been an obsession related worship bonding failure. Where there is a human related bonding failure the cravings drive a need to be captive and that must be granted, she needs to have her feeling of possession fulfilled and be encouraged to worship.

The feeling of possession is best maintained at all times for her. If you leave the house it is best if she is wearing a chastity belt, and locked in until her partner unlocks her again later so the obsession can be maintained.

A woman will adore her partner's attention and often play sessions will take place where she can role play an animal to enjoy her partners company. Dressing up and playing like a cat or dog. She also enjoys a lot of sexual stimulation. Again edging is very good, and telling her not to wear under garments or to simply strip can be a nice reward for both her and her partner.

Where a woman finds it difficult to give herself it is best to always allow her to pee for her partner, Mother Nature's submission, which will ensure her bonding equilibrium is properly aligned to her partner. She will always know she has to give herself and submit to her partner, and that giving of herself will allow the bonding to mature and encourage the worship state to happen. She can orgasm regularly for her partner but it is best to ensure she gets good orgasms that makes her pussy pulsate or squirt, remembering that weak orgasms are part of Mother Nature's ruination process.

Discipline, control and enforced obedience are used to help her serve and worship. Acts of worship like sitting at their partners' feet, wearing a collar, using bondage for submission and sucking cock for periods also allows her serve and worship. They can also extend their worship side to being made to beg which can be very intense for their bonding.

The issues here are her ability to be comfortable with a person who might be a stranger and work needs to be done to create a new belief system. Again porn sessions together can help build the trust that will allow her to be comfortable with her partner and her extreme narcissistic bonding and the more she wants this to happen the easier the adjustment will be.

The worship process is not extreme here as such, it is simply what Mother Nature wants to happen, so she can complete her worship bonding (or narcissistic bonding obsession) have her total happiness, enjoy her total humiliation, give her total submission and thrive on her total love and also enjoy the uplift in health that can be generated by this.

Brats who are at a much higher risk of needing extreme narcissistic bonding are also the ones at risk in failing to use extreme narcissistic bonding and finding worship with their new partner because of their single minded approach to life and their failure to achieve their worship and bond with their partner previously.

Brats who do not have a bonding equilibrium, find giving themselves very difficult because they can only give themselves properly in worship (or a bonding obsession), so if they are made to pee for their Master it will also make them give themselves in worship and it will help them. I have found that mature brats will often enter extreme narcissistic bonding relationships in their thirties, so they have been previously doing ruination for a good number of years before they arrive here, trying to combat their frustration, cravings and self-harming with weak orgasms often generated by their clitoris in the final stages to try and relieve the levels of frustration.

A brat entering extreme narcissistic bonding must hunt for someone she can worship and find that magnetic attraction that she knows she can be successful with and it cannot be any of her previous partners or her husband if she could not successfully engage her worship bonding system with them.

A total worship relationship is different here and she must be emotionally heightened and use importance instead to allow her to use an obsession. The emotional heightening will often happen by degrading because that is how her bonding systems are designed to work. She is aloof, self-important and of high standing so simple degrading acts heightens her emotional state.

This worship increases with the severity of the degrading and her love is generated as she is degraded. This has the unusual effect of allowing her to love a person more and more the more she gets degraded, but it also allows her to generate very high levels of bonding and worship when she is kept in an emotionally high state and driven by obsession.

This means that the more she can engage and connect with her partner the more her worship bonding is activated and micro-management allows her to stay in a state of worship and in a total obsession.

The partnership can engage in all sorts of fun that will heighten her and kindle her worship bonding. She can be taken shopping with a wet spot on her dress, or made to feel like a slut with no panties on or given a discreet Camel Toe (so as not to offend others) or Wedgie and she will love it.

It may seem bazaar, but if she is held in a degraded state 24/7 she will enter a total obsession and just float along. In this state she finds the purest love Mother Nature can give and her worship is given without conditions. She is totally degraded, totally in love, totally submissive, totally happy and able to enter a state few of us can imagine within her total state of worship.

For guys that like to be worshipped this is the ultimate relationship where it is less about looks and more about mental stimulation and you need a very strong mind here, basically you need to be as single minded as she is, where you dominate your partner, you look after her, maintaining her in her worship state and obsession.

As these are very talented females they will dress up and use artistic makeup to create the creature of your desire, you can write on their bodies, take them for walks with butt plugs inserted and other sexual activities that provide her with a strong emotional connection and of course being kept in a naked state indoors is degrading too.

The use of a little pain is also appreciated here and spanking can be used to heighten her for her bonding and orgasms, verbal degrading will help her too and you can tease her relentlessly and make her beg for your permission so she can orgasm. Activities like body art and wax play can also be fun for both and you can create a photo album which you can let her review regularly, which will also help her degraded state.

Personal hygiene is important of course and although there can be a lot of styles for pubic hair like a heart or landing strip it is perhaps better to consider that both parties are waxed to ensure everything is properly cleaned after play time (an epilator is now available too), the whole body is a good idea and then there is a good clean area available for the activities you use.

As her partner is repairing her worship bonding she can get some recovery for her health in time, but as we have seen this process is not something you can just terminate. Managing her worship state is crucial; failure to do this could lose all of the effort and improvement in her condition that has been achieved.

She should only bond once here of course and the extreme narcissistic bonding partner should always stay with her so she gets the best care, she must remain in a strong state of worship and she must not have her obsession start to deplete. Changing partners is possible of course but is best avoided so a stable environment can be maintained.

An accommodating environment can help her greatly here and pictures of her naked body parts placed around the house will help her a lot (which can be tasteful in guest areas), also if there are plenty of these pictures in the bedroom she can wake up and transition into an obsessional state.

There are a lot of toys that can be played with too, some have remote control and there is a personal vibrator alarm clock which is available (Little Rooster) which could be a great help when she wakes in the mornings. As well as using a chastity belt there are some more delicate and decorative types of G-String that are done in metals like a gold cage and position over the pussy area nicely and are very tasteful and I think look splendid.

What we are seeing here is that this relationship can be managed without the abuse or physical pain that is often associated with narcissism. The simple use of emotional heightening and importance is all you need to do to manage a narcissistic bonding obsession.

Both parties must realise though, that just as in normal narcissistic bonding when the woman's worship bonding is set by emotional heightening and importance the man's worship bonding is also set by emotional heightening and importance or obsession and that will be the same here.

That does mean that it is a good idea to match the potential life expectancy of the partners because of the impact of PTSD should one of the partners die and it is sometimes reported that strongly bonded couples can die together, so the responsibility to look after each other is extreme here.

Of course brats are not physically restricted as such and they can enjoy a longer life and entering into this type of symbiotic relationship can help provide good health for both parties.

This is the ideal situation but that is not always reality. Brats that choose extreme narcissistic bonding will often be slow entering extreme narcissistic bonding which leads to nervous system damage and they will often join a Master with several women in a harem. This needs to be an informed decision as there can be issues with a harem such as jealousy.

A shared environment will often lead to a more clinical approach where she does not get sufficient attention. She may be unstable in the mornings after sleep, her sleep patterns maybe unpredictable and she may be degraded in ways that don't accommodate her cravings. Males looking after multiple women can also feel they are suffocating and decide to leave which can be devastating for women who are worshiping. A harem is not always a good solution and how it works needs careful consideration.

Some of my experiences as a Master with women that wanted to train for extreme narcissistic bonding come next:-

A woman that became a brat a little later in life I connected with had developed brat biology and suffered a worship bonding failure, she found it very difficult to come to terms with her cravings and would not even describe them even to me. She was still in her early twenties and self-harmed regularly about once a month and had been suicidal a few times in the previous year. She had previous experience with Masters and was using them to help her with her orgasms. She loved activities that increased her emotional drive and edging could do that and she also peed for me each day.

In her training with me she quickly learnt how to do breast orgasms and she was able to do these even when she was on her period. She also learnt how to edge without touching and could do these anywhere, also including when she was on her period too. When I asked her if her fantasies were to be kept naked in a cage by my side and serve me she reluctantly said yes. Surprisingly perhaps, she was looking forward to that becoming a reality and wanted it to happen and the training she did improved her emotional state and provided a good improvement for her wellbeing.

It is just a shame that she had to feel so guilty about her condition when she is still a perfect woman for Mother Nature but perhaps less so in human society. Extreme Narcissistic Bonding is still a little down the road for her and there is little that can be done to stop it, society needs to be more open and accept these women to help them.

I chatted to and helped train others too and noticed how common it was for these women to be in their thirties. It also became apparent that some were in extreme difficulty because of their ability to get good fulfilment from their orgasms. Some of the physical characteristics I encountered were poor and even no feelings in the vagina making orgasms weak or non-existent. Others had only a small clitoris and too found that they suffered from poor arousal and poor sexual enjoyment. One woman was leaving her husband to seek extreme narcissistic bonding to rescue her from her sexual cravings, her fall into suicidal thoughts and I noticed she too had no feelings in her vagina. It was very apparent here that the lack of fulfilment in their breeding activities had limited their ability to bond as strongly as they might have and fully take advantage of Mother Nature's importance processes and drive their bonding obsessions.

Here it is a good idea to consider what can be done to improve their sexual enjoyment and a clitoris enlarger can be a good way to increase the arousal process. For the vagina Ben Wa Balls can be used every day which may bring some feeling back and an improved emotional drive from the clitoris might in time activate their vagina and connect them both up. If these do not bring an improvement it may be necessary to try sensory deprivation techniques to try and leverage and enhance their orgasms and their emotional wellbeing.

What seems to be clear here is that brats can be created after a bonding equilibrium has started to form and girls are capable of changing to brats beyond their childhood years.

For training I used the standard active bonding techniques which here were supplemented by further emotional heightening tasks which could introduce subjugation and control. I also introduced pet play where things like collars were worn and butt plugs used along with stimulators like nipple clamps and play activities were carried out to extend and increase the arousal process.

What seems clear is that women suffer more from their cravings when their mind is not occupied and they will work all day and cope ok only to suffer in the evenings. Occupying their minds for longer sessions of a couple of hours or so with a strong emotional stimulation allows their cravings to ease and their minds to settle. Full Extreme Narcissistic Bonding moves this process into a 24/7 environment.

Again what we see here is Mother Nature's belief system importance being carried out. The daytime allowed other activities to be carried out because they were important to her belief systems and generated her purpose in life during that time. Once that time had passed other belief systems needed to be gratified to maintain a strong emotional drive and pacify her belief system failure.

Another brat that discussed training with me was in her mid-twenties, she had self-harmed as a teenager and then entered a narcissistic relationship with a slightly older guy. He regularly abused her and she found that although he abused her she no longer self-harmed and she had accomplished a successful narcissistic relationship with him so she was willing to manage that trade off. However this relationship had eventually failed and they split.

The emotional impact was very severe and a week later she became paralysed down one side of her body and had to use a wheelchair. The doctors had not managed to determine the cause of the paralysis over the next three months and she was getting desperate to get a better understanding of her condition.

Clearly this appeared to be a nervous system issue and all of her other symptoms were also related to her nervous system but she was also taking anti-depressants and anxiety medications. I queried these and asked her what benefits these medications actually provided and she responded none, but the doctors had prescribed them so she took them anyway.

I think that people often struggle to distinguish PTSD conditions with other conditions and here we get to see the real impact on the nervous system that a worship bonding failure can generate and that is why women can become suicidal.

I was able to give here some constructive advice about narcissism and the way it can impact the nervous system and cause nervous system damage and how occupying the mind and emotional heightening or obsession would be good starting points for her to prevent further nervous system damage.

I would also suspect that Extreme Narcissistic Bonding here may arrest here deterioration and give her some recovery in time but how much is difficult to say.

The rules for Extreme Narcissistic Bonding are simple; a woman is degraded to maintain her obsessional bonding and this can be achieved without abuse if the two partners agree to an acceptable process which can deliver the importance that a belief system failure carves.

The interesting think about Mother Nature's extreme narcissistic bonding though is that for women that are not totally in an extreme state we can simulate extreme narcissistic bonding and generate a state of worship themselves in a midway point between Narcissistic Bonding and Extreme Narcissistic Bonding which we might call Extended Narcissistic Bonding.

We shall visit this next.

Extended Narcissistic Bonding

Before a woman has totally ruined her bonding she can enter Extended Narcissistic Bonding prematurely of course and relieve the failed bonding condition by using worship to set her bonding to join with her alpha male and satisfy her cravings. Here the extended narcissistic bonding environment is used to manage her life outside of a micro-management process which allows her to continue her daily life in nearly a totally normal way and here we take many of the aspects of extreme narcissistic bonding but introduce them into a more normal daily life.

The issue again here is her ability to be comfortable with a person who might be a stranger if she elects to use a Master and work needs to be done to create a new belief system. Again porn sessions together can help build the trust that will allow her to be comfortable with her Master and her extended narcissistic bonding and the more she wants this to happen the easier the adjustment will be.

This may include women with severe anorexia, anxiety, a bipolar disorder or depression, if she also has had a worship bonding failure or obsessional failure she may be suicidal. A combination of depression, anorexia and bulimia which can be deadly may mean that Extreme Narcissistic Bonding is Mother Nature's only option to find a remedy for that. These are often life threatening conditions and may have reached a point that is so severe that the woman wants to resolve them in extended narcissistic bonding.

These are serious medical conditions and women should consider an Extended Narcissistic Bonding before they are forced into Extreme Narcissistic Bonding or a total health failure.

When the bonding equilibrium has swung to an extreme position arousal is vital to ignite her sexual stimulation and her orgasms again and get her emotional balance heading back towards the centre especially if depression is involved and there is a low sex drive causing bonding equilibrium issues.

Here there are other tricks that women try too. You can understand why sufferers are naturally drawn to father figures for their partner, they are more stable and naturally provide a stronger level of bonding, they are more understanding and more comfortable using stronger levels of arousal play and they also naturally relieve the level of pride in a woman when she has an older guy on her arm. This can have a calming influence on an anorexic or a bipolar condition.

Using aids like a chastity belt or collar can help maintain a woman's state of worship as she becomes reliant on her alpha male to supervise her life. As well as a chastity belt there are some more delicate and decorative types of G-String that are done in metals like a gold cage and position over the pussy area nicely and are very tasteful and can also simulate a chastity belt like the erotic jewellery at therimbastore.com.

If there are concerns over how this will work you can write down the rules, which should also contain a safe word or gesture to stop activities if they become too uncomfortable, agree them and sign them so each party knows their role and responsibilities, how things will work and avoid any potential legal issues. It may be scary and you need to choose the right partner and older guys are far more suitable, but there can be light at the end of the tunnel which gives a woman hope, an incredible partner that looks after her and breaths life back into her again. And for a guy he gets the chance to shape the woman he wants, it is not only about what she is, but what she can become.

I have noticed that for males there are now dozens of chastity devices available, millions of them have been sold and they are very popular amongst the gay community. They can provide the control and sexual tension that allows a male to enjoy the emotional heightening and importance that they desire in a relationship; but I doubt they really understand what they are playing with and the consequences that can occur if their worship bonding is set and what then happens if that worship is abruptly terminated. These devices can be fun but they can also cause gay males to become suicidal if they are used and then dispensed with, and they may not understand what has caused the problem.

But one thing is clear; the use of a chastity device is exceptionally good at emotional heightening and driving importance, providing a controlling element for someone and subjugating them. Providing this helps them generate a narcissistic bonding obsession and helps them achieve a state of worship when they need to repair their bonding systems.

When it comes to resolving women's cravings or obsessions it seems there can be three levels of intervention and no doubt there can be shades of them that are most suitable for any given situation. Now we are entering a time when self-harming and suicidal thoughts for women are escalating at unprecedented rates making women aware of their options is vital to ensure they get the best opportunities for a happy life.

Female Stalking

There are thought to be around 7.5 million stalking issues in the US occurring each year and over a quarter of them are female stalkers, so around 2 million.

The standard rhetoric is that stalking is born out of rejection, jealousy and revenge, but I think that is an over simplification of what is actually going on. Stalking is very much a bonding issue, or should I say a failed bonding issue and this is not personal contact and submission for a sexual act, it is the other half of our bonding process, worship.

If I look at the suicide rates in the US, which are climbing sharply, around 20% are female but they are rising faster than men, and if you remove the figure for the veteran suicide rate from the male totals they approximately match up. That correlation is exactly what I would expect to see when a worship bonding failure is being born out.

As we know establishing our belief system can be a gradual process that is completed by experience, or a belief that is instilled into us by worship. When worship is used, that worship is a fundamental part of our live, a life force emotion which has established our purpose in life. It enables us to act as a group and perhaps a good example of this is Japanese culture where everyone is taught to worship the emperor and everyone acts uniformly and knows how to respect a humble approach to life, because they serve their emperor.

That is an extremely powerful culture that was able to supply unlimited soldiers and kamikaze pilots in the second world war who would give their lives for their emperor and they could act in the most brutal of ways to ensure the success of the emperor in battle. The US needed to use a nuclear weapon on Japan because they knew it would be impossible to take Japan with foot soldiers as everyone would fight to the death.

That power of worship is also used to initiate the bonding process with a girl's crush and their first bonding has the two elements, a girl's equilibrium is set to align with her alpha male so she can bond, orgasm and breed successfully and then her bonding obsession is set to form her unshakable belief in her partner. It is often said that you don't see a partner's faults when you are in love and worship is that part of the bonding process.

When partnerships break up that worship is abruptly halted and we incur emotional trauma, as one of our life beliefs, one of our most fundamental purposes in life, is taken away. It is no surprise that 44% of male victims are stalked by previous intimate partners. That type of emotional trauma causes us to do what we would never really intend to do. We need to find a way to maintain our worship or suffer the conditions that Mother Nature has dictated with a worship failure, total frustration and cravings which leads to self-harming and then becoming suicidal.

It is understandable that we try to repair this emotional damage to our bonding by finding a way to continue or replace our worship and alleviate this frustration in our lives. Again the figures show another 32% of the male victims are stalked by an acquaintance, and 11% of victims have been stalked for five years or more.

However, that 11% does show that the issue diminishes in time and proves that people do move on and establish alternative bonding in their life, a new worship and a new purpose in their lives. The victims of course can suffer issues themselves as they have uncertainty introduced to their lives and can suffer from anxiety if they feel their own bonding is being compromised.

This is very much a human cultural condition we have introduced to our society, society has added this complexity and some cultures are more prone to it than others. The more freedom we have the more chances we have to go wrong and we need to find better ways of resolving these issues.

If people understood what the issues were I feel everyone would be able to lead a much better life, and for people that need to resolve equilibrium bonding issues and worship bonding issues there are simple ways to get these in hand and under control. Narcissistic Bonding is not always readily available for women that have a worship bonding failure, but they must understand what they need and start to find a partner that can provide this.

We must remember though that a broken belief system and the emotional trauma that is incurred is largely a self-inflicted condition and it would not normally happen with monkeys. The solution to repair or create a new belief to utilise your worship too must be self-inflicted. Women that have trouble establishing a new belief system need to take advantage of hypnosis to establish an affinity and a new belief to establish their worship again.

Brats who are very single minded, selfish and stubborn, do not use their bonding in the same way as women who have normal two sided bonding and Mother Nature compensates for this with a stronger desire for worship. They want to complete worship tasks and they have a strong desire to serve. Because of their increased worship needs they are also more likely to have a bonding worship failure which is an emotional trauma and that initiates self-harming and then becomes suicidal when they are younger.

They are also more likely to stalk to fulfil their worship needs and when they get older they are also more likely to suffer from a Narcissistic Bonding failure and feel worthless without a purpose in their life and then become suicidal. Mother Nature will instigate her maximum worship craving to allow her to continue in her breeding cycle. When their bonding is in a totally failed state they need to enter Extreme Narcissistic Bonding to rescue their bonding and establish a state of worship with their alpha male who can use micro management and stabilises their bonding which gives them what they need.

For brats it is clear why they need new partners when they start craving for worship because they have not managed to worship their partners and become fully bonded. What is easily managed in nature is not so straight forward in human relationships where males do not acknowledge and cater for female worship unless they are narcissists.

Females that rely on a worship bonding in their relationships can become incredibly jealous if that relationship is in jeopardy and may go to extreme lengths to protect it or recover it and this is seen most vividly in stalking.

What is clear here is that women that stalk can use narcissism in that they have formed an obsession for a potential partner. That obsession will allow their worship bonding to stabilise and it will cure their cravings if they are brats. It can also stabilise other conditions that exist around their bonding equilibrium. But on the down side they will find it difficult to maintain an obsession and when it breaks, perhaps through rejection or isolation, they will get a worship bonding failure or PTSD and then be exposed to becoming suicidal. Other conditions related to their bonding equilibrium might also return. This makes stalking a very unstable approach to bonding and eventually it will always end with PTSD and narcissistic cravings if they do not find an acceptable relationship to replace the stalking.

The stalkers are the females that will often end up with Extreme Narcissistic Bonding needs because their acts are already taking an extreme course of action to resolve their bonding needs. When their cravings start to take hold and their behaviour pattern is already emerging and perhaps set for the future. When they enter Extreme Narcissistic Bonding they will emerge as full time stalkers in a narcissistic bonding obsession, worshiping their alpha male whilst they are micro managed and this is perhaps a journey to their fate. Perhaps this book will encourage those people to find a better solution.

Driving a narcissistic bonding obsession by stalking however does relieve bonding condition failures but this can only be temporary of course because such a dangerous action can cause territorial issues and women have been known to kill other women when their territory is encroached and aggressive stalking can lead to all sorts of complications. We refer to these as crimes of passion of course and narcissism, as we have seen, can cause violence and the trouble with stalking is it is not a permanent solution unless you form a full relationship later. Not only that, but women who have a bonding equilibrium subsequently need to use narcissistic bonding in future to maintain their narcissistic bonding obsession.

The stalkers are also suffering from a Borderline Personality Disorder as that is the new terminology which has grouped together the bonding failure conditions and the Borderline Personality Disorder condition parameters need to be extended to include stalking. These figures indicate that the earlier figures which are evolving still need to increase by two or three times to get the full scope of the condition in the US, as it will be the brats that are prone to stalking and of course they are in ruination when they do this. Women that use narcissism to stabilise their bonding equilibrium are already in ruination and using worship, so it is fair to say that all of the stalkers have entered ruination.

In a recent study in the UK of the last 350 women murdered over 90 percent of them were stalked by their killer. That is how serious stalking is and the issues that arise around a worship bonding failure.

Society needs a much better understanding of our worship systems to help alleviate this type of behaviour, stalking is not the answer.

Unstable Women

You probably wonder how I got into all of this and it will perhaps surprise you. Women with bonding issues are often severely driven to try and resolve their dilemmas. Women are known to be devious and here they can be very devious.

As you can imagine a brat that stalks will often try and win the guy she is stalking. She needs to resolve her worship bonding failure and she is highly equipped to do that. She is more single minded more authoritative, more organised and she wants to be dominated to facilitate her narcissistic bonding obsession. Her sex drive is far more capable than a normal woman and she can satisfy almost anything her partner wants when she enters such an obsession. She is just better equipped all the way around and she will often hunt the man and take the man of her choice, believing she is superior if she takes him from another woman.

I had some relationships with women that had severe bonding issues and it was a challenge to resolve their emotional traumas. Two of them had anorexia and I noticed that this condition was most prevalent when their emotions were running in a high state and I started to realise something. Their emotional balance was a key factor in anorexia and the use of humiliation (embarrassment) and orgasms to calm anorexia was not the complete answer and I concluded that other emotions were all also playing their part in swinging their emotional balance.

I started to increase my knowledge when I noticed some of the other females that were suffering with anorexia were also very vulnerable when they were in a high emotional state. When I combined my experiences with anorexia, my observations fuelled by other sufferers and my knowledge of emotional swings that I had accumulated with many years of working in the betting industry where emotional heightening was causing obsessions things started to form a picture.

There were a lot of questions and I was sure I already had many of the answers and that emotional heightening was the key, as I had already discovered that a high emotional state was the root cause of anorexia. As we have seen anorexia is also comorbid with anxiety which is also part of the bonding equilibrium system, anxiety is also comorbid with depression and depression is part of the bipolar disorder and these conditions and their connections are also confirmed there.

I decided to study BDSM and became a Master to work out more about what was going on and of course I already knew a lot. Women with these extreme conditions loved to be dominated and have strong orgasms generated and it was a lot more common than I thought. I learnt a lot more enjoying relationships with a lot of women and discovered the secrets of submission and degrading.

My relationships included a woman that had attempted suicide, a nurse with sexual cravings, then a woman that was pride high and then a manic depressive (bipolar) that had attempted suicide multiple times. I was able to improve their wellbeing and I also proved that you could generate emotions that were so powerful they could generate orgasms without anything stimulating the body, just by mind games alone. I worked with two rape victims and worked out their issues and also women who were struggling with suicidal thoughts, and then someone started encouraging me to write a book.

Some of my partners were incredible helpful too and were able to relate their experiences for their childhood which was also very helpful. You may be surprised at what comes next, but in the BDSM world these techniques are commonly used to help women with these types of issues.

Female Arousal

Everyone is a little different when it comes to humiliation (private sexual play), for example if I walk up to a woman donned in my cricket whites and said I want you to take your clothes off for me so I can admire your wickets, it would get all sorts of responses. Maybe a response like, I would like to play a few strokes with you and a couple of overs too would be what I wanted, but the likely slap might leave me totally stumped.

Sexy games between partners are a huge boost for us though and if I said the same thing again to my partner my desired results might be exactly what I wanted. Perhaps we might enjoy a play fight and then when the woman's arousal was ignited we would rip each other's clothes off.

Not only do we play simple games, we can play dares, set tasks and also cheeky humiliating punishments for something not completed on time or sometimes deliberately wrongly.

What we notice here is that humiliation has two sides of course, just like the sexual initiation; it can be highly arousing with a partner and also total embarrassment with a stranger. We see the two sides of an emotion, excitement and arousal and the self-consciousness in embarrassment, and a play off between the two to see which one we find the more dominant and it all happening in our minds and driving our emotions higher or lower.

Women love to spend hours getting ready such is their dedication to being a woman, displaying themselves in their skirts and high heels. This reflects how much they enjoy their feminine role in life and how much they enjoy sexual stimulation even in a fairly modest way.

Their clitoral stimulation is an extension of that sexual desire and when their guy goes down on them and uses his mouth it is that clitoral stimulation that drives them wild, it swells and then throbs until sometimes when they get penetrated and orgasm they explode; they find the orgasm just doesn't stop and it runs out of control, generating further orgasms and aftershocks for up to 30 minutes, which is a true enjoyment and some of the reward we get with a strong bonding with partners.

We feel things differently and how we use humiliation depends on how it turns us on. There is a further difference here between introverts and extroverts or exhibitionists. For the introverts they are happy with standard private play. An example might be pee, if I said you have to drink a full glass of water and then stand in the shower until the pee runs down your legs it would be embarrassing and hot as I sat there and watched you. But to an exhibitionist that would not be humiliating enough to drive her emotions and instead I would have to say kneel in the shower tray while I pee over you.

They like to feel the force of someone doing something to them and this is called degrading. Degrading is a much stronger form of humiliation which might include acts in public or being displayed on a porn site. Similarly, if I said pee through your panties on the toilet it would be humiliating for most of us, but degrading would be being told to go sit on the park bench or sit on the grass and pee through your pants, or walk outside until the pee runs down your legs.

We are just so different and partners need to experiment to get their humiliation just right so they can ignite the perfect orgasm. Little games will often help keep the sexual tension boiling and having a no panty day is always a favourite and leads to a little teasing as the day unfolds. Another might be holding a lipstick in your pussy and then using it on your lips, even both sets of lips.

There are toys also that can help spice the day up like Ben Wa Balls which are two balls joined by string and inserted into the vagina, they bounce up and down and make steps exciting, when you have to wear them when your partner tells you to, it can spice things up. For the anal enthusiasts there are butt plugs and butt plug sets for training, these can be very relaxing for someone to wear and of course if you go shopping with it in it livens the day up. Body writing can also be fun as well as you sit in front of your mother with slut written over your pussy mound and over your tits (this is under your clothes of course) and a little pain can heighten sexual activity too with women will often get excited by spanking.

There are other tricks you can try too, like if you struggle with clitoris stimulation you can rub a small amount of toothpaste or clitoris stimulation cream on your clitoris and get used to clitoris stimulation. This will help you start your edging if you feel it takes too long. Getting used to enjoying a swollen clitoris can be one of the joys of life for a woman and make her sex life so much more fun, even if you feel your vagina is too large to enjoy good sex there are vaginal balls that you can insert and hold in there all day which make you grip them and in a couple of months you can be tight again.

Women that find themselves in ruination and doing the orgasm chase will appreciate much stronger humiliation techniques and being dressed up as a baby and diapered can provide a strong sense of submission.

Brats will only usually submit to their partners using their bonding obsession and they are degraded. They prefer activities with a strong worship element and have their worship side pandered to, where discipline, control and obedience are used to help her serve and worship. She will likely enjoy being dressed up as a school girl and made to obey teacher. They can be made to obey and comply with rules that will challenge them like not being allowed to pee in the toilet. Brats also like to edge because it allows them to serve and they should always be made to report an edging event to their guy. Other acts of worship like sitting at their Masters feet, wearing a collar, using bondage for submission and sucking cock for long periods also allows them to serve and worship. They can also extend their worship side to being made to beg which is very hot for them too and being verbally degraded helps their orgasms too here.

In ruination brats will become submissive and get a Master to help them generate their orgasms which they find therapeutic, but if they do not worship their Master and create a narcissistic bonding obsession they just continue the orgasm chase until they get into severe difficulties with their bonding and if they do not find worship they will suffer the final consequence of a worship bonding failure and become suicidal. Once a brat reaches ruination she can benefit from becoming a baby girl, being diapered and enjoy the degrading while her worship side is encouraged.

A narcissistic bonding obsession is totally different to standard bonding where emotional heightening is generated by standard submission which is used to generate her orgasms. A brat without a desire to simply submit to a male needs to feel she is being controlled and subjugated to provide the degrading she needs and her high standing has been compromised and she has been placed into an emotional swing that heightens her and enables her to submit. The more she is degraded the bigger the emotional swing and the stronger her orgasms are.

Younger Girls and their Crushes

The passing of time has meant we have moved on from the 1950's household with the dominant male and submissive female. In modern societies we are encouraging females to stride out and achieve. That is increasing the risks around their bonding equilibrium which is linked to their bonding and breeding and suppressing a female's breeding cycle is not tolerated by Mother Nature. Tackling these issues is incredibly difficult to deal with once their pendulum starts to swing and rise.

In the UK (2015) there were nine deaths of girls related to self-harming, feeling worthless and suicidal thoughts, that happened despite the drugs used and the care programmes available. Ever more teenage girls are now entering care programmes at a cost of £800 per day, and it is incredibly difficult to deal with these symptoms when a girl's puberty commonly starts at 12 and her male counterparts are still immature at that age. Girls will often try to chase older boys to be their boyfriend, but these advances are rejected for such young girls which leave them without their desired partners. Their parents will often try to protect them too in their early years and attempt to thwart relationships for younger teenage girls.

Sometimes a girl's sexual awareness can be triggered by a totally innocent activity too like riding a bike with the saddle positioned to tilt up or horse riding with a tight fitting saddle which can both stimulate younger ages. Also, girls that become sexually aware can raise awareness in others too and spread idea's that should be reserved for more mature girls and once a girl has gone through puberty she will naturally enjoy displaying herself with short skirts, high heels and makeup, as her sexual awareness increases.

A girl's first crush is an entirely natural event and she has a strong instinct built into her to go and obsess over her alpha male and complete her bonding. As we have seen such an obsession interacts with a girl's bonding equilibrium and bonding can then take place.

This can even be an unattainable male like a pop star in our society, where tens of millions of girls can join fan clubs and worship their idol on twitter and other social media. But if this bonding subsequently terminates it becomes a failed bonding (and a band breaking up can cause a nasty spike here too) and once that bonding process has been activated she becomes vulnerable. Her bonding can become compromised from an early age in our society and she may be held back several years before her bonding can be secured with her first boyfriend. She will deny Mother Nature's breeding process and suppress her bonding causing her equilibrium pendulum to rise to the high side.

Mother Nature will not allow the suppression of her breeding programme and her encouragements start with a hypomanic or manic cycle where she will get strong sexual feelings. The hypomanic or manic state is noted as having an increased energy or activity with a euphoric mood but also extreme irritability and poor concentration levels. These can be accompanied by an unrealistic self-belief along with poor judgement. Sometimes these episodes include drug abuse and proactive and aggressive behaviour and of course a denial that anything is wrong.

If the suppression continues and the girls elevate themselves with pride and a push to achieve, the pendulum continues to rise too as their bonding becomes totally suppressed and that escalation continues with anorexia, anxiety and insecurity. Because a crush is initiated by an obsession for their belief system and there is a failed obsession element then Mother Nature's frustration will also commence and introduce self-harming as the girl's frustration levels grow and she tries to find an emotional release. A girl that cannot breed is worthless to Mother Nature and if she does not yield eventually she will force her to crave and become suicidal.

It is now estimated that there are three pupils in every class doing self-harming, a figure that has doubled since the 1980's.

In 2014 there was a 70% increase in 10-14 year olds attending A&E for self-harming over the previous two years and it is thought that 13% of girls will self-harm at some point between the ages of 11-16. Given that is around four million females this translates to around 85,000 girls a year will start self-harming. The total figure for girls self-harming will be much higher of course given that some girls will self-harm over multiple years, so perhaps double that figure will be actively involved in self-harming and they are also 100 times more likely to commit suicide in the future. Of the 85,000 it is estimated that well over 3,000 will go on to cutting or burning, and well over 2,000 of those will then attempt suicide, the majority of those will attempt suicide multiple times.

It has been noted that these girls will often be the more well educated ones and the middle or upper class, so the ones who are most likely to elevate their status and perhaps least likely to masturbate to help themselves release their emotions and improve their bonding equilibrium. Vanity in girls and their mothers who often set the examples is a deadly sin here. A recent study has shown that only 58% of 17-year-old girls and 66% of 18-year-old girls masturbate.

Furthermore, a girl who crushes on a pop star is creating unrealistic aspirations in life. The romance of the pop star cannot be matched by the once local heart throb stacking shelves down at the local supermarket and she no longer feels submissive towards him. This will also elevate her status and suppress her bonding leading to bonding problems. A rising equilibrium starts with a hypomanic and then a manic cycle which can also trigger anxiety and if they are ignored it then follows on with anorexia; a worship bonding failure will generate severe emotional trauma with self-harming and a feeling of worthlessness followed by suicidal thoughts.

Once a girl's equilibrium is rising anything that stimulates the level of pride, whether it is defensively or acclaimed causes a deteriorating condition. So family arguments, fallouts with friends or partners, or being praised all cause pride heightening. Deflating activities like walking the dog with a poopascoopa, cleaning the toilet, sucking family member toes or simply writing a journal about the illness are all very therapeutic and cause a reduction in pride levels, an increase in bonding with deflating emotions lowering the bonding equilibrium. Taking a step back and remaining more humble in life is what is needed.

Of course any activity that increases your bonding with your family, friends or partner is very good. Stress should be avoided as it can act as a trigger to self-harming events due to the existing levels of frustration in a worship bonding failure.

The use of artificial aids for orgasms like vibrators will help release the emotional frustration and they can be very therapeutic, but of course this too is an unbonded sexual activity and will not provide the fulfilment aspect to get the maximum benefit on the bonding equilibrium. This eventually this will encourage a girl to start chasing orgasms and needing ever more intense humiliation to ignite her orgasms to benefit her bonding equilibrium. This could then lead her into bonding difficulties for the rest of her life.

Stubborn single minded girls that are brats, who do not have an emotional drive on their bonding equilibrium do not have rising pride levels and do not suffer from the pride heightening, or getting depression, mania, anorexia and anxiety, but they still suffer from frustration, self-harming, and become suicidal with a bonding failure.

That is because the obsession side of the crush can set their worship bonding and no doubt why a crush uses our highest level of bonding to initiate bonding, it works for both the bonding equilibrium and narcissistic bonding. Brats are more naturally dependant on their worship side for their bonding which is driven by a full bonding obsession and should ideally only bond once this way, but if their bonding fails abruptly they suffer a worship bonding failure or PTSD. A strong masturbation schedule does help to relieve the frustration condition but because their bonding equilibrium is not suppressed their orgasms can remain stable which is slightly different to a pride escalation issue.

However, a brat being single minded will also not be able to train with peeing to reinstate the bonding equilibrium side of her bonding because she did not possess an emotionally driven bonding equilibrium to begin with. This is an area where a stronger submission solution may be needed to manage her orgasms like bondage in the long term. Brats often do not see bonding as something they need to pursue and instead may look to get a partner that helps to increase and strengthen their orgasms to manage their condition. However, she can only repair the worship failure with another bonding obsession and that is difficult for younger girls, who are still too young for a worship relationship and narcissistic bonding.

Her orgasms initially remain unaffected after the worship failure as she is not connected to a bonding equilibrium. However, her orgasms are a little more fragile than orgasms that have the benefits of a bonding equilibrium and can use arousal more easily to ignite their orgasms. Her orgasms have to be generated without a bonding equilibrium and the benefits of easy arousal, without her bonding obsession and without being degraded and made to beg, which makes her orgasms more unstable and they become swamped by the belief system failure and rising frustration. They cannot generate the therapeutic emotional releases they need as the condition escalates and she is forced to engage in self-harming to relieve the frustration. She may fight it for a few years, but with her unreliable orgasms this is a losing battle and she will become suicidal. These girls basically need help and there is simply none available.

The recent studies have concluded the situation is getting much worse and escalating quickly, with numbers close to doubling between 2012 and 2015, which perhaps goes hand in hand with the digital revolution and a girl's ability to crush on celebrities who can promote themselves in an ever more intense fashion. A real concern when girls can get online at very young ages now and be exposed to celebrity glamour at a very impressionable time of their life.

Of course the vast majority of these girls will simply mature and enable their sex lives and bonding process as Mother Nature intended but many will also be left with bonding difficulties which will stay with them throughout life. Education may help them cope in their maturing years. That education has to start with their parents and schools. Mother Nature's breeding rules are not just a sex education; we need to educate for better emotional management too, to look after our youngsters, Health and Safety for kids.

Historically of course Hollywood's attempt to create an artist's fan base was limited to magazines and TV shows as well as the films and music. Perhaps a poster for a girls wall too, but that has all changed. Digital streaming has allowed the artists to circumvent parental control and they can unleash all of their glamour and romance directly into a girl's home.

Obsession is encouraged by the celebrities, and our worship bonding systems control the most powerful emotion we have and it can be a deadly force when it is unleashed on an unsuspecting public. Quite recently a tragedy occurred when a fan shot the singer Christina in the US and then himself. That is the level of force that worship obsession can invoke in people. Why would we let our children be exposed to that level of emotional intensity when typically, they do not have the same level of worship to guide them and counter balance that from other areas these days. The exposure becomes a total controlling factor in their lives.

I have seen pop stars with over 40 million twitter followers and using just the average figures, that amount of followers will generate over five million girls who will start to self-harm when they retire or they decide to get married and the crush eventually breaks for those girls. That will generate over 200,000 girls that will self-harm to the level of cutting or burning and over 125,000 girls that attempt suicide. These girls can be as young as ten and they have had their life hijacked, their bonding ruined and they may suffer for the rest of their lives. Of course the average figures will not apply here because these are the very girls that are likely to crush and have their crush broken, with unrealistic aspirations in life, the true figure might easily be double that of the average. That would produce over 10 million girls starting to self-harm, over 400,000 girls that will self-harm to the level of cutting or burning and over 250,000 girls that attempt suicide as they struggle with the consequences of the emotional turmoil.

If I look at the popular male sex symbols on twitter the total followers registered are now over 10 times that figure and a huge liability for female health. Of course I realise these figures are slightly speculative, but I have to approximate these figures to gauge the size of the potential issues.

The younger girls are very vulnerable and have little defence against this type of indoctrination obsession and once they are engaged they have little chance of escape. They cannot help themselves and this is a one-way ticket. Some cultures go to great lengths to protect their females and their bonding even using chaperones, but even they are now totally vulnerable to these online indoctrination obsessions. As digital technology continues to govern our lives it would not surprise me to see eight year olds becoming the targets of digital media and we will see those figures continue to grow.

Of course there is a fine line between indoctrination and obsession and even though this worship has been driven by pop stars they will rightly point out that it cannot be indoctrination if only 25 percent of the girls are infected, it must be an obsession on their fans part. That is true of course, what they have done is to create emotional heightening and how this impacts girls will vary and some will not be impacted at all.

What we see is here is emotional heightening generating importance, their belief systems being programmed to accept this as part of their life and to accept fulfilment as part of this process. Mother Nature's narcissism has been used for bonding, emotional heightening and importance generating control and subjugation and once it has been used it must always be used because that is how narcissism works.

But if we look at the other industries that create emotional heightening they are known to generate addictions and obsessions. So for example the gambling industry is strictly regulated, they warn participants not to become obsessional and of course it is limited to people over 18 (gambling addictions are now at record levels too). Other industries that rely on emotional heightening like the porn industry are also restricted to people over 18.

What the celebrity and pop industry is doing is using emotional heightening on younger girls that are not warned and they are not aware of the potential consequences and that is why there are such a high percentage of sufferers.

Parents are not being warned about the potential impact of digital indoctrination and the risks that go with industries that use emotional heightening to generate our entertainment.

What we have seen in anorexia is that activities that impact us in an emotionally heightened state cause compulsive behaviour that we recognise as obsessions and anorexia is the ultimate proof as to what is happening here. What we can also understand is that addictions, obsessions and indoctrinations all come from the same source, our worship bonding systems and they are all broadly equivalent but they have different initiation paths.

What is also clear is that it can affect us in varying degrees, just like drugs have categories A, B and C and they are graded on the strength of the addictions associated with them, they too are obsessions that are held within our worship bonding systems and they are generated by emotional heightening, emotional intensity and importance.

If we continue our comparison with drugs we can that self-harming can be a mild condition or a major condition and also that suicidal thoughts can be a mild condition or a major condition and perhaps we should think of cannabis and heroin when we assess the potential impact on a victim.

The addiction, obsession and indoctrination conditions are all the same with a different label, they all come under the indoctrination umbrella because that is what we accept as the process that manipulates our worship bonding systems historically. When the indoctrination breaks we have a fallout situation and that is what generates the withdrawal symptoms.

What we have also seen here is how vulnerable humans are to emotional heightening and a sustained emotional heightening activity can easily set our worship bonding if we believe it to be important. As we can see these conditions do not have to be stigmatised as a mental health issue, they are an emotional illness and we should treat them that way.

Another thing that is more than apparent here is that society likes to be entertained and we use emotional heightening to do that and it has tremendous risks for us. Not only with entertainment but we elevate and admire people, especially girls, and we cause emotional heightening in them and this can also contribute towards conditions like a bipolar disorder and anorexia.

In fact if we remove the 25 percent here that suffer from obsession what we see is that the other 75 percent are exposed to sustained emotional heightening without importance and that can impact their bonding equilibriums which leads to a hypomanic or manic conditions and then that exposes them to a bipolar condition, or even worse anorexia.

A recent survey has shown that nearly 25 percent of 14 year old girls have suffered from depression. That figure is of course way too high and shows how much our bonding is disrupted now we have introduced digital technology and have come to rely on it.

Of course there can be many reasons for depression and when we feel a break in our bonding we suffer from grief. But one of the most damaging is when a girl is in an emotionally high state like hypomania or mania and a stressful event or an event that causes rapid emotional heightening and then a crash, can cause a bipolar swing.

There has been a lot of media coverage about how digital media bullying causes serious emotional damage to our younger generation, which of course should cause anger and sadness for a couple of days, but instead it causes emotional trauma. It would seem here that a lot of the emotional trauma will be caused because a bipolar event has been triggered and that is what we are seeing.

These issues were not as prevalent in previous generations; they are very much a product of our fast flowing modern day digital life and we are now seeing how vulnerable we are to Digital Indoctrination and Digital Indoctrination Fallouts, along with heightening that causes long term emotional damage with both the bipolar and anorexia conditions. Because this is happening to us with our use of digital technology and it did not happen previously we must put these conditions down to the enhanced emotional heightening that is caused by digital technology. As we will see, this is also apparent in other digital entertainment products too.

What I would say is that strict regulation of how emotional heightening is used is urgently required now or the digital age will become a very dark age indeed.

Society is changing and it is not always for the better. If we fail to educate ourselves and look after our bonding, we are on a very slippy slope. Youngsters that can start to bond as young as ten years old and sometimes even younger, need protection from this digital onslaught too.

This is a very sensitive area to deal with given the vastly different cultures that exist around the world. If we take a look at the age of consent for example. In Austria, Italy and Germany the age of consent is 14; in Sweden, France and Denmark it is 15; Spain and the UK 16. Meanwhile in Turkey and Malta, teenagers have to wait until they are 18 for sex to be legal. This type of disparity only leads to further complications when a girl's bonding equilibrium is compromised.

No younger girls were used during the writing of this book, but I did chat with girls who had described their emotional experiences when they were younger, this included girls that had self-harming issues after been pop star fans and of course the news is full of emotional issues encountered using digital technology. Here we can start to understand exactly what is happening and anorexia itself is the proof of what happens during sustained emotional heightening and the formation of obsessions.

Gaming

Of course there are activities which may introduce obsession and indoctrination into our lives; but we can also obsess about something ourselves, until it becomes all-consuming and an indoctrination process and we see this as an obsession.

The biggest risks are from things like gaming which can captivate children especially, when they are at a vulnerable age. Obsessions like these become addictive and cannot be just simply withdrawn once an indoctrination process has formed. At least such an obsession is not abruptly terminated and when obsession occurs there is always the next generation of software to look forward to.

Activities that are obsessional and become self-indoctrinating like gaming will set a girl's worship bonding, but in the case of multi-player gaming and games with social interaction these are big communities in themselves. They provide a good connection with the other gamers and are a strongly bonded community with valid bonding for a girl's bonding equilibrium which should not end abruptly. The real risk here is when a girl walks away from her gaming with her worship bonding set that is not a natural use of her bonding. She will not understand that she has to use worship in her future relationships or suffer from an obsession failure, which may induce self-harming and becoming suicidal.

This community for gamers may not apply to low budget games and single player games, which can set a girl's worship bonding and release a girl's equilibrium pendulum and leave her exposed to an emotional disruption. There are well over

100 million single player gamers playing daily and approaching 50 percent are female.

Once an indoctrination has formed and a girl's worship bonding set there is not a valid bonding value in gaming for her bonding equilibrium. As gaming is based on competition, pride and achievement once the equilibrium pendulum is released it can trigger a rising equilibrium and all the associated issues that can happen with hypomanic and manic episodes and all that adrenalin may push the bonding equilibrium even higher and the pendulum will continue to rise to anorexia.

The worship bonding side will not be impacted unless there is an abrupt termination of the gaming, if that happens then self-harming and suicidal thoughts may follow. This activity could also create brats of course, who simply bond with themselves using the obsession if this gives them for a sense of self-importance in younger children and could be a reason that hybrid brats are created.

Clearly girls with a bonding equilibrium were never meant to use a bonding obsession for their bonding, except for their initial crush in monogamous relationships, their belief system should always be set subsequently by experience and a standard level of love after that. That process allows them to change partners and their alpha male during life more easily. Introducing a bonding obsession and worship into our normal bonding process is not how a normal balanced relationship should work.

Women who are monogamous with bonding equilibriums are raised in a human society and do not normally have their worship bonding set beyond their initial crush and do not always have the instincts to engage in a relationship driven by a bonding obsession. A woman who finds herself with a worship bonding failure will need to use Narcissistic Bonding techniques to introduce worship into her partnership.

When a brat plays a multi-player game or a game with a strong community she can exist quite happily as long as her worship bonding is set to herself and she can happily except the worship of other players.

The real issue for brats is that if they obsess about their gaming they will set their worship bonding and may then find it difficult to maintain just as in human relationships. This can lead to an obsession failure and which could eventually cause self-harming and becoming suicidal. Brats may not realise that they have encountered such an obsession failure and need to initiate a narcissistic relationship to correct their bonding.

Gaming is a popular pass time and how we use it can vary. For example if you take a young woman who is newly married with a baby it is unlikely that her gaming will ever become important enough to detract from the care and love she gives to her husband and baby and her mind is closed off to the intrusion from the gaming which does not become an obsession.

But if you take a young woman who is newly married without a baby and her husband is working away from home her gaming activities can be different, she can get drawn into completing the next level and setting and completing targets within the game if she finds she has time on her hands. Her mind is now open to the influence of the game and she can get drawn in to establish importance until an obsession forms as the constant images bombard her mind.

If this gaming is not part of a community this will lead to a hypomanic condition, then a manic cycle and possibly anorexia when her bonding equilibrium releases due to the invalid worship bonding value of a computer game for her bonding equilibrium as her obsession progresses.

Even though she is bonded with her husband, her husband cannot overrule her emotional drive established by the obsession unless he establishes narcissistic bonding for her too. If she reaches the final conclusion of her game she will need another game to maintain her gaming obsession, or perhaps to start the game again, but if she does not find an adequate replacement she will then get an obsession failure as her obsession is broken.

The issues here are that these women and girls are exposed to sustained emotional heightening that can not only cause obsessions but also impacts their bonding equilibriums which leads to a hypomanic or manic condition and then that exposes them to a bipolar condition, or even worse anorexia.

Here again we can see the issues around entertainment and emotional heightening and the way the introduction of digit technology has caused a substantial uplift to our emotional heightening from the games we used to play a generation ago. The real issue here is that parents do not understand the impact emotional heightening and importance is having and they are not being warned about the potential impact it could have on their children.

Clearly it is now time to give our parents strong guidelines to enable them to supervise the use of digital technology on our younger generations.

I have observed emotional heightening during gaming activities and know people who have become obsessional during gaming and of course it can be seen on the TV now with gaming competitions. Emotional heightening is our best entertainment but not warning people, especially those under 18, of the potential consequences of using sustained emotional heightening is dangerous for the users.

What we see is here is emotional heightening generating importance, their belief systems being programmed to accept this as part of their life and Mother Nature's obsessional forces of control and subjugation used and once it has been used it must always be used because that is how obsessions work.

A recent survey in the UK showed girls between 16 and 24 with nearly a 20 percent self-harming rate and at an age where this this condition should be decreasing it is still increasing. That is a strong indicator of emotional heightening in the digital world and not only how much self-harming is being generated but how much more bipolar and anorexia we can expect to see in this generation in the future.

Gambling

I have included gambling here not because there are huge numbers of female gamblers (maybe bingo), but because it introduces our perception of morals and a legal framework for dealing with similar entertainment industries that use sustained emotional heightening.

The bookmakers firstly are restricted to punters who are at least 18 years old and that is where we draw the line for emotional responsibility. This of course is seen in other areas of our life like porn, voting, drinking, joining the armed forces and getting married, this is when we are adults and responsible for our own emotional management.

We often try to help and guide people in their adult life, warn them of pitfalls and provide helpful advice to help them have an enjoyable and productive life and it has been largely successful. We can look at society and we can be proud of our achievements because we have established a governance process which largely caters for all of our society human needs.

You probably think I know little about gambling but I will surprise you, I was a betting office manager at 18 years old and remained so for over 10 years, so I do understand entertainment and emotional heightening.

I was able to watch emotional entertainment every day and the way we can derive enjoyment in so many ways. Most of the punters were very sociable and very entertaining in themselves and it was a pleasure to know them. I can still tell you that 8/13 represents 61.5 percent of the market. This is quite straight forward really, if we take 5 runners and make them all 4/1 and placed a pound on each we would get back our five pounds regardless of the winner. So we know 4/1 represent one fifth of a market and 20 percent. We also know that if we reverse the odds in a two horse race we get 100 percent, so if 4/1 represents 20 percent 1/4 must represent 80 percent. When the odds totalled up to over 100 percent the book was over round and the bookmaker could expect a profit, when it totalled less than 100 percent the book was over broke and he could expect a loss. Yes, I became an expert in risk analysis and statistics too before I became a computer programmer.

It was quite an education, but I got to watch and deal with people every day that were using entertainment and emotional heightening for their pleasure. The different intensities of that people could generate depending on how much they could win and also watch people that used to love to run up their winnings by increasing their stakes the more they won and increased their emotional heightening as they went.

It was a great experience, but I can tell you a story about the entertainment industry that I discovered myself, greed. We had to monitor punters who placed large bets or might be making a profit. I had one such punter who came in after pay day every month and spent several hundreds of pounds over the first week or two before he lost and vanished until the next month.

One month he started to win and increased his stakes and continued to win until he was betting a thousand pounds at a time on the horses. Soon he was over ten thousand pounds ahead and my race room controller was going berserk. He waited until he placed a few losing bets and was only five thousand pounds ahead and then told me to bar him from the betting shop.

I was almost in shock, a regular customer who lost five thousand pounds a year was to be barred because he was five thousand pounds up. I reluctantly did it; I was so humiliated as I explained that head office was declining any more bets from him.

That was one of life's lessons about the entertainment industry, they are only there to take your money, do not expect them to care about you or take a long term perspective, they just want customers who give them money.

That policy had also extended to the few customers who had developed obsessions and became compulsive gamblers. We did nothing to help, we just took their money. People will point out that has changed over the last 30 years and now there are help lines and there is a structure in place to advise people.

Of course the problem of obsessional gambling has not gone away and given these customers are responsible adults we would expect the problem to be under control and declining. That is not the case though and a recent study has found that there is now a gambling addiction reaching new record highs and almost an epidemic.

Some punters have become so addicted to playing roulette on the Fixed Odds Betting Terminal machines, dubbed the crack cocaine of gambling, they have simply lost everything and there have been a number of reported suicides because of gambling addictions. The interesting thing is that these crack cocaine machines are using the same techniques that we using in gaming, visual images with risks and rewards and they are noted as being highly addictive in government reports.

An estimated 2.3 million people in the UK are either problem gamblers or at risk of addiction, according to the industry regulator. Now that figure is over 6 percent of the gamblers in the UK and demonstrates what the entertainment industry, using emotional heightening, does to us and these punters are responsible adults over 18 years of age knowing what the risks are in advance and have a strong emotional counterbalance to not lose their money.

If you need proven facts from official bodies, morale judgements or legal governance it is found here already in the gambling sector and they too are looking at a huge boost in business with the advent of digital technology and are also generating substantial record numbers in gambling addictions and obsessions with 430,000 punters in the UK being classed as addicts.

Bulimia in Women

It is estimated that there are 30 million people in the US with eating disorders and between two and three million people are self-harming. Of course those figures are quite a multiple on the UK which is thought to have around 1.6 million people with eating disorders.

In the US anorexia has the highest fatality rate of any mental illness and eating disorders are a daily struggle for 10 million females (1 million men) and it is thought that 2.5 million women suffer from bulimia. Interestingly bulimia is given a higher percentage here than anorexia (62% to 38%) so nearly twice as prevalent as the 1.5 million anorexia suffers, with binge eating disorders accounting for the rest.

Bulimia is often thought of as an obsession that causes binge eating followed by a purge cycle using laxatives or vomiting. Because bulimia is driven by obsession it is simply the other side of the bonding system coin, whereas anorexia is driven by the bonding equilibrium, bulimia is driven by the worship bonding system and this is worshiping the need to remain thin and attractive and purge food.

A simple observation here seems to point to a possible progression as these figures are surprising, maybe I would expect to see these figures the other way around with anorexia the more dominant. I suspect that it is likely that girls who visit pride high and initially start with anorexia, then may become obsessive and paranoid about their appearance and also have a much increased chance of then becoming obsessive about their weight and eating; that may then lead to a bulimic condition.

If I reversed these figures it would point to a potential one million woman that have entered a bulimic condition by progressing through anorexia first and up to half of the anorexic females also get depression, so perhaps there are as many as half a million women with a major and potentially deadly health care condition in the US with a combination of anorexia, bulimia and depression.

As it is possible that females can be anorexic and bulimic at the same time as these are driven by different bonding systems, generating pride while they are bulimic can be very dangerous and trigger a combined anorexia and bulimic condition.

Brats though do not get anorexia and an obsession about their weight and eating will always lead to them becoming bulimic and this will also become part of their journey into ruination and potentially becoming suicidal with the bulimic condition.

What we see is here is emotional heightening and intensity generating importance, their belief systems being programmed to accept this as part of their life and obsessions being formed which generate a compulsion which cannot be broken because of the importance that has been attached to this activity within their belief systems.

Women who have a bulimia obsession can use the Narcissistic Bonding techniques to alleviate the obsessive condition and repair their worship bonding systems.

When you consider the combination of depression, anorexia and bulimia which can be deadly Extreme Narcissistic Bonding may be Mother Nature's only option to find a remedy for that. Brats who have used obsession to create their bulimic condition may also find that Extended Narcissistic Bonding or Extreme Narcissistic Bonding is a wise cause of action to correct their worship bonding as there are no medications available.

Looking at the age related figures for bulimia it is noticeable that there is a wide age spread, even into women over 50 and it would seem that when women need a cause in their life, dieting is an easy one to pick as it enhances their appearance and sexual attraction and this can lead to becoming obsessional about their weight.

As you would expect self-harm is a common comorbid condition affecting 34% of those with bulimia and as with the other worship bonding fallouts here too we can see that women who try to cure their bulimic condition or fail to maintain their worship condition fall into the trap of a worship bonding failure. Also, as you would expect there is an increased risk of suicide among those with bulimia nervosa and suicide is a common cause of death for bulimia sufferers.

In some ways Bulimia is very special though because it cements all of the pieces together regarding narcissism and our worship bonding systems, here we see the same compulsion and cravings that we see elsewhere and it activates the same withdrawal symptoms of self-harming and becoming suicidal that we see in the other areas of Mother Nature's obsessions and narcissism. It is the ultimate proof that obsession is narcissistic but we see it in another guise here and it is just the same as we see in gambling and other areas of obsession and it is all a part of Mother Nature's importance.

It is also unique because of the way women who had anorexia can use their obsessions to control their eating and get bulimia and as we have seen these obsessions are borne out of a high emotional state, emotional intensity and importance. It is also clear that Mother Nature's intention for anorexia sufferers is the control force of narcissism. So where there is a controlling force that is a compulsion and it causes cravings as withdrawal symptoms resulting in self-harming and becoming suicidal it is all part of Mother Nature's narcissism which is driven by importance and fulfilment.

Clearly this is a severe problem for the bulimia sufferers and just like the others that have an obsession failure, repairing their worship bonding here needs to be done by a new obsession or by increasing their partner bonding to a worship status and using Narcissistic Bonding techniques or Extended Narcissistic Bonding.

OCD in Women

It is estimated that there are 6.3 million people in the US with OCD (Obsessive Compulsive Disorder) or 2.3 percent of the population and just like other obsessions these are driven by our worship bonding. In the UK it is estimated that 1.2 percent of the population suffer from OCD and that equates to around 750,000 people who are currently suffering from the condition.

OCD is seen as a totally different condition to bulimia, but of course it is really just the same, a compulsion that must be served once it has been established as part of our worship bonding. These compulsions vary wildly from cleaning the house room by room in a certain order to people obsessing about their work or pleasure activities. As we have seen earlier, indoctrination sets our worship bonding and here we set it ourselves purely by obsession.

Of course OCD is comorbid with many of the other bonding issues like depression, bipolar, anxiety and anorexia and that is not a surprise. Many of the obsessions do not conform to a genuine bonding scenario and when the bonding equilibrium cannot accept it as valid bonding, it releases and then is subject to swings with our emotional turmoil.

Self-harming and suicidal thoughts are also common with OCD as you would expect and although I could not find any statistics, I would expect the level of self-harming to be a lot less than the 34% which bulimia victims suffer from because the obsession allows you to eat and there is not the strong temptation to avoid the compulsive condition.

Again, what we see is here is emotional heightening and intensity generating importance, their belief systems being programmed to accept this as part of their life and obsessions being formed which generate a compulsion which cannot be broken because of the importance that has been attached to this activity within their belief systems.

Women who have an OCD obsession can use the Narcissistic Bonding techniques to alleviate the obsession condition and repair their worship bonding systems.

When you consider the combination of depression, anorexia and OCD it will not necessarily be deadly like bulimia, but Extreme Narcissistic Bonding may be Mother Nature's only option to find a remedy for it, if it is a serious condition. Brats who have used obsession to create their OCD condition may also find that Extended Narcissistic Bonding or Extreme Narcissistic Bonding is a wise cause of action to correct their worship bonding as there are no medications available and OCD is a potential route to becoming suicidal for them.

As with other worship bonding failures cravings occur if the compulsive disorder is not being serviced. A recent study showed that nearly 12% of OCD sufferers attempt suicide and around 1.5% of sufferers die from suicide and this appears to be approximately half the rate of the bulimia sufferers.

Clearly this is a severe problem for the OCD sufferers and just like the gamers who have an indoctrination fallout, repairing their worship bonding here needs to be done by a new obsession or by increasing their partner bonding to a worship status and using Narcissistic Bonding techniques or Extended Narcissistic Bonding.

Anorexia in Women

In the US anorexia has the highest fatality rate of any mental illness and eating disorders are a daily struggle for 10 million females (1 million men) with the figures predicting 1.5 million women suffering from anorexia and around 2.5 million women suffering from bulimia with the binge eating disorders accounting for the rest, around 6 million women.

Anorexia is our most deadly of the mental illnesses which perhaps accounts for perhaps half a million fatalities every year. For those with persistent anorexia about 20 percent die within 20 years and 10 percent die within 10 years and little is understood about anorexia beyond this book.

Anorexia is a terrible illness to live with as it restricts the victims eating capability causing them to vomit after meals, sometimes hours after they have eaten. These sufferers often find themselves eating very light meals during a prolonged anorexic spell in order to get some nourishment. Commonly they will eat things like fish, high sugar items in order to generate some energy and ice cream is also a favourite.

Not only is the eating cycle disrupted but they can get severe anxiety as well making each day a substantial challenge. There are further dangers here too, an obsession about eating can easily trigger a bulimic condition. Bulimia is thought of as an obsession that causes binge eating followed by a purge cycle using laxatives or vomiting where food is eaten but the digestive cycle is avoided in order to remain thin and attractive.

Anorexia is often associated with the younger females and bulimia with women of any age and it seems likely that the older we get the more control we have over our emotions and the less prevalent anorexia becomes with mature women more likely to be bulimic.

The real issue though for anorexia sufferers is if they get depression as well and a low sex drive condition. With weak orgasms it is already difficult to maintain an emotional balance in life and release and exhaust their emotions. Once depression occurs extended arousal sessions become necessary to ease the depression and generate the orgasms that are necessary to be able to eat again. Maintaining a strong sexual stimulation to stop the depression is vital and stronger orgasms will help generate a better emotional balance.

Women who have persistent anorexia can successfully use the Active bonding techniques where they can enjoy enhanced sexual stimulation and also alleviate their anxiety and high pride condition to get their emotions back under control and enjoy a much better life with a potential much longer life span again.

Anorexia sufferers are also prone to get obsessions and what we see is here is emotional heightening and intensity generating importance, their belief systems being programmed to accept this as part of their life and obsessions being formed which generate a compulsion which cannot be broken because of the importance that has been attached to this activity within their belief systems.

This is Mother Nature's narcissism being generated within the emotional high condition and humans should not try to use obsessions that are undesirable. They are better using the Narcissistic Bonding technique to alleviate the obsession condition and in extreme cases they need to consider the Extreme Narcissistic Bonding option too.

Clearly our emotions are a major part of growing up and maturing, letting them run out of control can give us major problems. When our emotions run high with an infusion of pride it becomes a serious issue and this is what causes anorexia. Adults are more likely to be able to resolve these emotions by balancing them in their daily lives and exhausting them as Mother Nature intended. These emotions are not as easily resolved in our younger generations who struggle to balance and exhaust their emotions until they take a partner and start their breeding cycles as Mother Nature intended.

It would seem that once a woman is prone to being anorexic she will always be prone to that condition and must take extra care during her life to manage and balance her emotions more carefully to prevent the condition returning. Becoming obsessive about food and eating is dangerous and can lead to bulimia.

A combined illness of depression, anorexia and bulimia is incredibly dangerous and a severe problem for the anorexia sufferers who need to deal with the bulimia obsession or obsession failure too. Repairing their worship bonding here needs to be done by including a new obsession or by increasing their partner bonding to a worship status and using Narcissistic Bonding techniques, Extended Narcissistic Bonding or Extreme Narcissistic Bonding in extreme cases.

Depression in Women

It is estimated that there are 40 million adults in the US suffering with anxiety or 18 percent of the population. This is consistent with other surveys, like in the UK where a recent survey showed nearly 20 percent of adults admitted to suffering with depression or anxiety disorder. Nearly one-half of those diagnosed with depression are also diagnosed with an anxiety disorder.

Of course depression and anxiety might also be relative to how people relate to their financial health and social wellbeing and people will often feel down and anxious when they are struggling to make ends meet. Clinical depression is a more accurate way of measuring our true state of health.

More accurately depression affects approximately 16 million Americans, or 6.7% of the population in any given one-year period. Depression is the leading cause of disability worldwide, and is a major contributor to the overall global burden of disease.

In the US they were 16 million people (2015) in the US that suffered at least one major depressive episode and the figures suggested in various surveys show the women are more far prevalent with depression making up twice the percentage of the men, with some surveys showing women make up to 80 percent of the total for depression with the Borderline Personality Disorder condition.

However, the real cause of depression in the major depressive disorder figures is biological and the figure of 10-12 million women who suffer from a major depressive disorder have become emotionally unbalanced and endure a state of emotional turmoil.

The depressive state is noted as having a sad and empty mood, with feelings of hopelessness and a loss of interest in pleasure. There is a decreased energy level with poor concentration levels and decision making along with restlessness, irritability and pessimism.

Depression is a terrible illness to live with as it can make life seem unbearable at times. Sometimes victims retire to bed to endure it for a day or more and life can be very difficult. Women I have helped with depression will go to extreme lengths to ignite their orgasms again and sometimes heighten their emotions to get a stronger orgasm to relieve themselves from the depression cycle.

What is clear is that a depression cycle is triggered by a subdued state that then subdues the sex drive, or a subdued sex drive. In this lower subdued state it is harder to lift your emotions back into a positive state because of the low sex drive condition and lack of euphoria.

The edging training worked exceptionally well with a woman that suffered from depression because it initiated arousal and her sex drive then lifted the depressed state so she was able to regain her normal emotions again and generate healthy orgasms again.

Women who have persistent depression can successfully use the Active bonding techniques where they can enjoy enhanced sexual stimulation and also alleviate their anxiety to get their emotions back under control and enjoy a much better life. Depression sufferers who also get an obsession will be better using the Narcissistic Bonding techniques to alleviate the obsession condition as well.

Clearly our emotions are a major part of existence and we need them functioning normally to maintain our own life balance. Adults are more likely to be able to resolve these emotions by balancing them in their daily lives and exhausting them as Mother Nature intended. These emotions are not as easily resolved in our younger generations who struggle to balance and exhaust their emotions until they take a partner and start their breeding cycles as Mother Nature intended.

It would seem that once a woman is prone to suffer from depression she will always be prone to that condition and must take extra care during her life to manage and balance her emotions more carefully to prevent the condition returning. Hypomanic and manic episodes along with anxiety and anorexia can be waiting for those that allow their emotional state to rise out of control.

Bipolar in Women

It is estimated that there are 5.7 million adults in the US suffering with the bipolar condition or 2.6 percent of the adult population. This is consistent with other surveys, like in the UK where a recent survey showed two percent of adults admitted to suffering with the bipolar condition.

The bipolar condition is thought to have a roughly equal split between men and women and is deemed to have two sides of an emotional state described as a hypomanic and manic episode and a depressive episode and these have been characterized to bring clarity to each of these episodes. However, as we have seen, it is possible that both the hypomanic and manic conditions may also be accompanied by depression too.

The manic state is noted as having an increased energy or activity with a euphoric mood but also extreme irritability and poor concentration levels. These can be accompanied by an unrealistic self-belief along with poor judgement. Sometimes these episodes include drug abuse and proactive and aggressive behaviour and of course a denial that anything is wrong.

The interesting thing about the bipolar state is that if you can curb the manic sexual invigoration cycle to allow the depression to flow through in a more sedate way you don't have to over shoot into the depression cycle and suffer the low sex drive condition which then needs heavy sexual stimulation to lift the condition. Severe bipolar sufferers can spend hours trying to stimulate themselves to pull back out of the depression cycle.

The depressive state is noted as having a sad and empty mood, with feelings of hopelessness and a loss of interest in pleasure. There is a decreased energy level with poor concentration levels and decision making along with restlessness, irritability and pessimism and is the direct result of a low sex drive manifestation from the manic cycle where too much emotional depletion was generated.

Depression is a terrible illness to live with as it can make life seem unbearable at times. Sometimes victims retire to bed to endure it for a day or more and life can be very difficult. Women I have helped with depression will sometimes go to extreme lengths to sexual stimulate themselves to ease the depression and ignite their orgasms again and sometimes heighten their emotions to get a stronger orgasm to help relieve them from the depression cycle.

Bipolar women I have helped have sometimes been driven to orgasm binges to release their emotions when they are in the high or manic state and this of course leads to rapid heightening of their emotions. Later they then find they suffer from the drop that follows which generates another depression cycle. Also, this leads to the orgasm chase and initiates ruination which starts a whole new set of problems.

The two sides of the bipolar condition can be seen in the pendulum we looked at earlier. What we see are women who rise towards pride high through the hypomanic state and manic state. This side of the pendulum cannot be sustained for long periods without a severe reaction from the sufferers emotion stability and of course anorexia and anxiety are there waiting as well and the state becomes unbearable.

A high sex drive is generated to try and release and exhaust the high emotional state and allow the pendulum to swing back down to a more central position, but stopping bang centre is not something that we can do when an emotional swing starts. We see the swing continue to drop below centre and then into a new depressive cycle.

This swing will now start all over again as the pendulum starts to rise as the drop starts to ebb away. We will of course try and help generate excitement and high spirits to get back to the former state and often this will be supported by the use of drugs. The climb continues and a full swing has completed. Alpha females can easily fall into a bipolar condition.

Women who have a persistent bipolar condition can successfully use the Active bonding techniques where they can enjoy enhanced sexual stimulation and also alleviate their anxiety to get their emotions back under control and enjoy a much better life. Bipolar sufferers who also get an obsession will be better using the Narcissistic Bonding techniques to alleviate the obsession condition as well.

It would seem that once a woman is prone to suffer from a bipolar condition she will always be prone to that condition and must take extra care during her life to manage and balance her emotions more carefully to prevent the condition returning. This condition and the swing is very difficult to stop and very easy to start again.

Anxiety in Women

It is estimated that there are 40 million adults in the US suffering with anxiety or 18 percent of the population. This is consistent with other surveys, like in the UK where a recent survey showed nearly 20 percent of adults admitted to suffering with depression or anxiety disorder. Nearly one-half of those diagnosed with depression are also diagnosed with an anxiety disorder.

Of course depression and anxiety might also be relative to how people relate to their financial health and social wellbeing and people will often feel down and anxious when they are struggling to make ends meet. Anxiety is also used to categorise some of our phobias like claustrophobia and sometimes used in conjunction with a compulsive disorder which has been born out of obsessional behaviour and these are not purely anxiety related but might be triggered by anxiety or might trigger anxiety.

Anxiety is more clearly thought of and more accurately thought of clinically as a condition which instigates fear, worry, apprehension and nervousness. What seems clear is that just like we can generate a subdued emotional state and lower our sex drive and then get depression, we can also generate anxiety by our emotional state and anxiety is directly linked to our bonding systems. Anxiety is driven by feelings of isolation and vulnerability.

Anxiety is an emotion characterized by worried thoughts and feelings of tension which can include physical changes like increased blood pressure. People with anxiety disorders usually have recurring intrusive thoughts and worries leading them to avoid certain situations when they become concerned. People who have extreme anxiety can become withdrawn from the worry and fear being constant and overwhelming which can be disabling and lead to a life of isolation.

Anxiety is also comorbid with depression and of those diagnosed with anxiety nearly half are also diagnosed with depression. Mixed anxiety and depression is the most common mental health problem in the UK accounting for 9.7% of adults. It is no surprise that anxiety is also commonly linked to the hypomanic and manic cycles and anorexia too.

What is clear in the statistics is that a lot of other conditions referred to as phobias are also included in the anxiety bucket. Other obsessions and disorders are often also grouped in to the anxiety figures and these are not strictly anxiety related. We need to be clear that phobias and obsessions like OCD are totally different and should not be considered as part of anxiety and anxiety will most often go hand in hand with our bonding equilibrium irregularities; depression, manic and anorexia and anxiety is directly linked to our bonding systems. My experiences with anxiety have always shown a lack of confidence with emotional instability and poor bonding often accompanied by poor and irregular sleep patterns.

Anxiety is most commonly associated with depression but can occur whenever we enter a state of emotional turmoil. The hypomanic and manic cycles, anorexia cycle and the depression cycle can be accompanied by anxiety and it is a good indicator that our bonding processes are unstable, but it is not always when our bonding equilibrium pendulum is swinging with other conditions. It is very much an indicator that our emotions are unstable and our bonding has suffered and is in jeopardy.

Generating a calming emotion for anxiety is not an easy thing to do, but what is also clear is that when a woman exposes her peeing activity she naturally generates anxiousness as she would crouching down in the long grass before civilisation and exposing herself to a potential attack by predators. When instead this is done with a partner an emotional swing is generated and the initial anxiousness is then replaced by trust and security, as these emotions take precedence anxiety is quelled naturally. Of course, when a partnership generates trust and security this is a natural basis for love and this then strengthens the love in the relationship and the bonding process.

Clearly our emotions are a major part of existence and we need them functioning normally to maintain our own life balance. Adults are more likely to be able to resolve these emotions by balancing them in their daily lives and exhausting them as Mother Nature intended. These emotions are not as easily resolved in our younger generations who struggle to balance and exhaust their emotions until they take a partner and start their breeding cycles as Mother Nature intended.

It would seem that once a woman is prone to suffer from anxiety she will always be prone anxiety and the other accompanying conditions and must take extra care during her life to manage and balance her emotions more carefully to prevent the condition returning. A manic episode and anorexia can be waiting for those that allow their emotional state to rise out of control.

Conclusion

I think Mother Nature's bonding process is a truly remarkable biological event. If we were monkeys no doubt it would work perfectly for us and I especially appreciate the differences she can create when she uses worship and a more standard belief system level of love to generate the bonding strength. It might be expected that she would use a girl's crush, a form of bonding obsession to generate a girl's initial bonding under normal circumstances. As they say, your first love is your big love, the one you will never forget.

We fall in and out of love the rest of our lives and when the bonding process is successful a woman's equilibrium is correctly aligned to her partner and her humiliation and orgasms create a successful breeding environment within her relationship.

When women end up in ruination doing the orgasm chase because they have suffered an acute bonding failure Mother Nature again allows worship in Extreme Narcissistic Bonding to secure a woman's bonding and gives her another chance to have a stable relationship with her alpha male.

Of course there will be a lot of people that believe the answer to a bonding and breeding issue is simply to have a baby. But unfortunately it is not that simple, around 15% of mothers do not bond as they should with their new baby and the love and bonding does not develop. Brats that are self-important and need a bonding obsession can also have a negative attitude to the pregnancy and fall into this category. Whereas anxiety (which can be associated with a both a depression or the hypomanic and manic cycle condition) during pregnancy can produce postnatal depression and a bonding failure. Furthermore, mothers who fail to bond with their new child suffer from behavioural issues with their child and it can become an escalating issue. This postpartum bonding needs to be addressed with strong bonding techniques during pregnancy.

Although there is no further research to call on a figure as high as 15% would suggest that the other groups with adult bonding difficulties also have child bonding difficulties too. Bonding issues go much further than a woman's adult relationship and they continue into her family life. Having a baby can be a nightmare for a woman that cannot bond with her child. A pregnant woman is wise to make an extra effort during pregnancy to increase her bonding activities with her partner and the bonding activities of the family unit so that this feeds through to the new born baby too.

Another observation here is that up to 80% of females will suffer from mild depression during their first year as a mother and of course this is a time when they will have a reduced sex life when they are a busy mother with lower sexual stimulation and a lower sex drive. That loss of emotional balance can allow their bonding to drop and depression will follow, and having a baby does not mean you can ignore Mother Nature's breeding cycle.

And of course any girl that relies on an artificial form of sex without being properly bonded, like riding horses or using vibrators should not be surprised if they suffer from a swinging bonding equilibrium. Artificial sexual activity depletes your bonding fulfilment and the orgasm chase is waiting for the careless.

Human society has imposed its own rules on sexual activities and they don't always synchronise with Mother Nature. Her punishments for breaking her bonding and breeding rules with depression, manic episodes, anorexia, self-harming and ultimately becoming suicidal are understandable when you consider our prime reason for being on this planet. It is her reason, not ours and she is ruthless with the way she enforces her creature rules. Proper bonding is essential for breeding females.

This is a sensitive area, but humans have always evolved. We have encountered these issues as humans and we are all equally to blame for that. The important thing is that we do not look back at our mistakes but look forward to a better way of doing things. Humans can evolve and be successful when we put our minds to it. Bonding issues may be complex but they are not insurmountable and I have proved we can move forward if we have the will to succeed. Every society will view solutions differently so I think those discussions may vary.

But to those who put their head in the sand and hope the problem will go away I will say the problem is escalating and the situation is getting worse everywhere I look. How many girls, sisters, daughters and partners will have to die every day until we will tackle the problem?

Men too need to step up to the plate, we have been guilty of not looking after our women's breeding needs and it is our responsibility to look after our women properly and ensure a woman's bonding is properly taken care of. Quality time and personnel time needs to be replaced with bonding time. It can be such fun too.

When I checked the number of suicides in the US it was rising sharply and has climbed to over 40,000 a year and surprisingly the boys were at a level around four times that of the girls, but with the girls rising fast. It is notable that the largest percentage of male suicides are the veterans accounting for 20%, or over 20 suicides a day. Of course when young adults answer the call of duty they are engaging in something they played throughout their childhoods, something they believe is either death or glory, as the way to fight and serve their country.

Joining the military can enable their childhood dreams and engage them in emotional heightening. When they leave the military of course, if they have obsessional, they have their worship status terminated when they return back home. If soldiers, who become obsessional, then have it abruptly taken away there can be serious consequences for those people, as we have seen people become suicidal when their obsession is abruptly terminated and their purpose in life is taken away. This condition is often referred to as PTSD (posttraumatic stress disorder).

These people who no longer have a cause in their life also become available for indoctrination by others of course, who may have a totally different agenda and it might not be such a surprise to see such a soaring spiral of violence and mass murders now taking hold in the US and around the world. What is clear is that when an obsession is used to control our emotional state and then that worship is abruptly taken away we lose control of our emotional state, become unstable and that condition can lead us to become suicidal. Introducing Extended Narcissistic Bonding as an alternative worship regime would save a lot of lives here and provide the purpose people need in their lives again and prevent many of these suicides.

It is not only the military that generates an obsession and worship in this way, athletes also become totally obsessed with their competitive goals and nowhere demonstrates this more than the Olympics. They train to take part in and achieve the pinnacle of their careers here and once that event is over the obsession and worship collapses dramatically. The worship that has been sustained for a number of years ends and a craving to work out and bond is unleashed to replace their training regime and the previous bonding with their sport and coaches. Their sexual activity is rampant in an attempt to satisfy and repair the failed condition in their belief system. In 2016 there were 450,000 condoms supplied to just over 11,500 athletes or just under 40 each, quite a number when you consider they actually share these between two people, over a 16-day period. Athletes appear to be a very high risk group to worship failures when they retire.

Of course these activities may introduce obsession and indoctrination into our lives; but we can also obsess about something ourselves, until it becomes all-consuming and an indoctrination process.

When people are feeling suicidal gaming may offer a life with worship if they find they are able to obsess about it. Military personnel may find this very therapeutic and even a direct substitution for war like activities that can satisfy their obsession. The online interaction should also be able to link military people back to their comrades and reinstate their brotherly bonding. Of course to repair a fundamental belief system failure and the emotional trauma that is encountered you have to believe in something, have an affinity with it and also be prepared to be obsessed with it to establish a new belief system.

That is what it takes to build a new belief system and repair an obsession failure. With the Extended Narcissistic Bonding this is imposed on you and hard wired in to you by a partner, but here it is a purely mental process and as a worship failure is mainly self-inflicted you have to find a solution that you can also self-inflict. You need to be happy that it is something you can have a fundamental belief in, be obsessed with it and you must also satisfy the bonding element that has also been lost as part of the solution. If there is no such affinity then this solution cannot work, however as this is a belief system again hypnosis can provide that belief and affinity to establish a link into a new worship culture for those that wish to try it.

Reading books, which can also become obsessional and can erode a girl's family bonding as they will have less interaction generated with others. They will get emotionally involved with the books and enjoy being elevated to a status of hero, this can lead to elevating a girl's bonding equilibrium and the potential issues that can cause, also a brat can be created with self-importance at an early age.

Another digital revolution that can cause obsessional behaviour is social media. Some people have addictive habits that lead them to regularly post and then check the number of likes that they get. This type of anxious behaviour is also to resolve bonding issues and as we have seen anxiety is one of the symptoms that bonding issues cause. On social media they able to fulfil their need to feel liked and be part of a community. Similarly, there are people that feel a strong desire to comment on all of their friend's posts to feel part of the community. Social media of course can also appear as a stalking activity and it is important that a bonded community is maintained, the highest levels of anxiety ever recorded for children are now prevalent in schools and of course anxiety is a bonding issue and likely to be driven by social media content.

Other recreational spectator sports like wrestling and football also generate a number of girls that crush on the stars and run the risk of a bonding failure.

Of course there are many occupations besides the ones we have looked at that involved authority and have the potential to cause a rising bonding equilibrium leading to becoming an alpha female and suffering from a hypomanic or manic episode, a bipolar condition or worse. Some of these are Police Women, Prison Guards, Scientists, Doctors, Nurses, Models, Lecturers, Judiciary, Politicians and the girls taking part in Broadcasting to name but a few and it is important for these groups look after their bonding.

Young girls can also bond quite well with pets, which can also give a lot of comfort and friendship, but these are less suited to adults who can derive a lot of friendship and comfort but only a limited amount of bonding. Of course there are women that try and intensify that bonding by carrying the pet around with them and they can become obsessive about their pets in this way and gain with their bonding stability, but I know women that still go pride high who have pets.

The more I have looked into this the more I have concluded that bonding and breeding is the meaning of life. Mother Nature placed us on the planet with a few simple fundamental rules, organise security, eat and breed. Security and eating are also fundamental to our bonding and assist our bonding but the breeding cycle cannot be broken, those are her rules. We are not able to brush them aside and it perhaps it would follow that the ordinary girls with a bonding equilibrium feel insecure and get anorexia along with extreme sexual thoughts when their breeding fails and they go pride high. That of course applies to all species, when breeding fails the very reason for us being on this planet also fails. The fact that salmon near Seattle now contain cocaine and antidepressants is not what Mother Nature intended.

Given the similar figures for bonding failures in teenagers and adults it is likely that bonding difficulties stay with a girl throughout her life and she needs to maintain her bonding to keep her bonding in place. Couples will often share the bathroom and a woman should take the opportunity to pee in front of her guy as often as she can as this is a brilliant way to secure and enhance your bonding. A woman will only pee in front of a man if they are bonded and that is a bonded activity.

It is noticeable we had a much more stable existence going back in time where our lives and emotions were much more synchronised with Mother Nature and we were closer to monkey's. Today's complexities in life and the emotional strains that are placed upon us have driven us in a new direction that is moving us further away from Mother Nature and creating conflicts that we struggle to resolve and the digital age is placing additional emotional stress on the way we live and those pressures can be damaging our emotional state.

Romance is one of Mother Nature's incredible gifts in life and it is a spark that stays with us throughout our lives. Anything that dims this process is not considering Mother Nature or Mother Nature's retribution when this goes wrong.

Mother Nature has provided us with two bonding processes and they are each available individually in a monogamous relationship depending on our biological makeup. Where there is a leader of the troop like in monkeys and he wishes to control breeding he can enforce worship on his troop to control the female breeding cycle, that way the evolution train gathers momentum, as it is always the strongest and wisest that leads. Of course the females will always submit to him or they will break their worship and then suffer a worship bonding failure and become suicidal.

Equally all young females will copy their mother and learn to worship their leader too. When there is a leadership challenge and it replaces the troop leader the females must all worship the new leader, any renegade female that refuses will again suffer a worship bonding failure and become suicidal and then crave for their worship to be reinstated. It is possible to project that the leader will chose when he will reinstate them with his narcissistic bonding which they are forced to accept. Equally, when the queen is replaced and her worship is rejected she too will suffer a worship bonding failure and become suicidal and then crave for worship and perhaps she will then be forced into Extreme Narcissistic Bonding too. It seems truly amazing how once such a society is established Mother Nature perpetuates it and enforces its structure through the generations with the troop leadership changes generating the new DNA required for evolution.

The bonding equilibrium is emotionally driven but appears to be part of the immune system which maintains all of our organs. That includes the female monthly cycle of course and the strengthening of the immune system after a woman has had sex in preparation for parenthood. As the immune system is very much physically and emotionally driven you could speculate that the orgasm contractions and spasms and our emotions actually notify the immune system of the sexual act and of course that is what women in ruination find difficult to achieve. But the real clue is the fact that anti-depressants and anti-anxiety treatments work with the immune system and the connection is confirmed there. Anorexia of course can generate depression which is also part of the bonding equilibrium system and that connection is also confirmed there. Also, when the bonding equilibrium goes into ruination the immune system also weakens and exposes women to an increased risk of illness and diseases like cancer and lupus.

Our worship systems are totally separate of course and they are controlled in our minds and by our nervous system and that is why there is no medical cure when you become suicidal. You can of course take mind altering substances that might alleviate the condition.

Some drugs and alcohol can also be used to start an obsession and then impose themselves onto our worship bonding. You can envisage this is the case because when the worship bonding systems are set by obsession and they generate cravings when they fail. The interesting comparison with drugs of course is the various levels of intensity for the condition and the strength generated by the cravings when the substance is not available. Of course using such a substitution to stabilise a worship bonding failure would only generate a new dependency and it would not be a type of worship that could set a valid bonding value in the bonding equilibrium and life's shortening cycle would still continue.

These girls are fundamentally normal girls that have generated a sustained and intense emotional high (or obsession) in their lives and a bit like drugs and alcohol which also generate highs in our lives, they have incurred withdrawal symptoms. They endure frustration and cravings until they use pain and self-harming to create an emotional release. Often it is very difficult for them to recreate the same emotional intensity that created the condition to alleviate the condition and return to a normal life with their worship bonding systems back in harmony again. Another issue here is that it is possible to over feed cravings and intensify them which can cause the condition to deteriorate.

It seems that potential indoctrination risks for our worship bonding systems directly correlate to the risks that we see and the impact that we see using drugs and alcohol and we need to manage those risks in exactly way. Other mental illnesses like OCD and Bulimia are all caused by the same obsessional type of activities and trigger a strong drive and craving to complete the desired worship tasks.

Substantial emotional releases caused by corporal punishment (which can release endorphins), the infliction of pain, extreme exercise or strong orgasm generation can all ease the frustration and the pressure on the nervous system, but they are not a cure and the use of orgasms will continue ruination.

Big Pharma will no doubt find a drug to promote for the more serious suicidal cases, but although this can be mind altering it will have to be an addiction that lasts 24 hours a day for a brat or they will simply get their cravings back and continue their journey onto becoming suicidal. Other females using drug addiction will find it releases the bonding equilibrium and they will be exposed to hypomanic and manic episodes and perhaps depression too. Drug addiction will not provide an acceptable solution and Mother Nature's wrath for such a use may not be seen until future generations. Recently I have also noticed that there are now reports of 20,000 children with abnormalities because of women using Valproate which is often used for treating a bipolar condition.

It seems clear that we have to use Mother Nature to cure a worship bonding failure and return to either a tribal or cult style of worship or worship a partner. Worship is simple to achieve, we must submit and enslave ourselves to acknowledge our worship state by performing acts of worship which register in our minds as an acceptance of the superior controlling force and completes our worship bonding. The strength of these acts will often depend on our ability to accept the controlling force combined with the state of our bonding systems, which is why people who find it difficult to submit end up in Extreme Narcissistic Bonding and the brats in particular, with their high standing, have a catastrophe when they suffer a narcissistic bonding failure. But, if your partner is able to generate acts of submission and obsession he can also dominate you and allow you to worship him and cure your worship bonding failure with Mother Nature's narcissistic bonding. If you struggle with this a chastity belt can help you establish your narcissistic bonding.

Clearly promoting digital technology to the heights of tribal leader in our bonding processes has huge implications for all of us and there is Virtual Reality (VR) now appearing on the horizon which may prove to be even more immersive and obsessive. Mother Nature has given us that self-determination of course, but it is perhaps a frightening way for the human race to evolve.

We all fall under Mother Nature, she rules humanity and every creature on this planet, but on reflection it seems Mother Nature does have everything under control. As you would expect she has placed a ring of steel around her bonding processes. Mother Nature is just so far ahead of us we don't even see it, but she is there, monitoring and guiding our civilisation. The different levels of bonding that are available to us are remarkable in themselves, from a standard boy meets girl type of relationship to Active Bonding or a Narcissistic Bonding approach, Extended Narcissistic Bonding and Extreme Narcissistic Bonding itself all work successfully if we follow Mother Nature's path to cure our bonding ailments. Worship and the way we use our fundamental belief system is also a truly remarkable way for us to impose governance on our lives and be successful as the human race.

The real concern is that if we use self determination to become more unruly in our personal lives, chase pleasure and deny our bonding, we use drugs to maintain our self-esteem. If we continue down this path we are creating the ruination of the human race. It would appear that Mother Nature understands this, do we?

Depression has an estimated 350 million people affected worldwide (perhaps up to 80% female, or 280 million) and there are over 800,000 people die due to suicide every year, which is nearly 20 times the US figure above. That is the scale of the problems we are dealing with now in the digital age. For eating disorders if I scale up the US figures there are around 30 million anorexia sufferers and for bulimia there are around 50 million sufferers of which 17 million engage in self-harming.

A worship bonding failure is far more difficult to deal with than the bonding equilibrium where there are simpler corrective measures and also medications available for depression and anxiety. There are no medications available for a worship bonding failure and yet if we go on creating high levels of emotional heightening in our entertainment and Digital Indoctrination Fallouts at our current explosive rates we will see self-harming become as common as depression too in a generation or two.

What this research has indicated though is that people who suffer from all sorts of PTSD conditions that have being caused by worship bonding failures can look to narcissism as a potential solution to resolve their dilemma. What is also clear is that all of the emotional conditions that can cause a worship bonding failure can also cure a worship bonding failure providing there is sufficient emotional heightening, intensity and importance to match the failure, but we need to try and avoid the more undesirable obsessions.

It also seems that our belief systems are established and then regulated by Mother Nature's importance which is driven by our emotions. The higher the emotional drive and importance we place on our belief systems the more Mother Nature helps us regulate our beliefs and uses our emotions to monitor this. We establish our meaning of life through these varying intensities of importance. This process enables narcissism and enables us to control our lives and our destiny. It might be said that it is the fundamental driver for intelligence too.

Of course we just call human bonding that relies on our belief systems narcissism, but in reality Mother Nature's importance is everywhere in our belief systems. It makes us steadfast or stubborn, it creates different levels of compulsion and we refer to these in different ways, like habits, addictions, obsessions, indoctrination and worship. Narcissism is just the human side, but it is the way humans can repair belief system failures by generating emotional heightening, intensity and importance to establish a human bonding obsession.

Once we have repaired our belief system we must maintain our importance to maintain the cause in our lives otherwise we will become frustrated and worthless again. That is how life exits and how we evolve.

Mother Nature has not left us without resources to successfully manage our emotions and it is not surprising that when it comes to our bonding systems she insists that we manage our bonding emotions correctly to secure the continuity of the human race, but when we stumble we can easily correct these and pick ourselves up again.

For the bipolar condition women and girls are becoming ever more exposed to sustained emotional heightening through digital technology. This is not only in the areas of pop star fans and gaming but it can be seen in all areas of digital technology like gambling where addiction is now at record highs. We love our entertainment and the emotional heightening that goes with it but sustained emotional heightening exposes us to the hypomanic and manic cycles of the bipolar disorder and that can lead to a full bipolar condition developing.

Anorexia too does not have any medications available and when patients are put under stress they naturally defend themselves with their pride and this needs to be effectively managed by those that look after anorexic sufferers. Anorexia is effectively death by starvation of some of our brightest females and should not exist and we need a much better understanding of this high emotional state.

Clearly there is a severe issue with sustained emotional heighten and when that causes severe bonding ailments we need to improve the emotional management techniques we use in our bonding processes.

Humans now need to make emotional management a priority before we end up in a total mess. When I step back I realise just how much our emotions mean to us, they are the very life force within us and without them we would be automatons and effectively lifeless or more like insects living life by instinct alone. I hope this book will help women value their emotions and understand that good emotional management gives us life, take it, it belongs to you and you have a right to good emotional health.

Thank you and good luck with your bonding.

Please like and share.

Author: Paul Tempest